Home-cook and devotee
Elizabeth Hodder wrote *The*
a natural conclusion to year
family and friends. A forme
Equal Opportunities Commission – and a firm
believer in making cooking accessible to
everyone – Elizabeth brings here a common
theme of the shared love of comfort food.

She lives in Cambridge with her academic
husband and within baking distance of most
of her family and friends.

'Both a practical cook book and a look at the
history of tart making' *Financial Times*

'More than 80 recipes, many old, some
thoroughly modern, all laced together with
chewy chunks of domestic history' *Food & Travel*

'Scrumptious' *Mirror Magazine*

'Some cookbooks are for looking through and
leaving on the coffee table, others have recipes
which shriek "Try me!", and *The Book of Old
Tarts* definitely comes into the second category'
Cambridge Evening News

'The perfect stocking filler' *Scottish Field*

FOR DICK

THE BOOK OF
OLD TARTS

Over 80 scrumptious sweet and savoury recipes

Elizabeth Hodder

headline

First published in 2001
by HEADLINE BOOK PUBLISHING

First published in paperback in 2002
by HEADLINE BOOK PUBLISHING

10 9 8 7 6 5 4 3

ISBN 0 7472 3034 X

Typeset by Letterpart Limited, Reigate, Surrey

Printed and bound in Italy by
Canale & C.S.p.A.

HEADLINE BOOK PUBLISHING
A division of Hodder Headline
338 Euston Road
London NW1 3BH
www.headline.co.uk
www.hodderheadline.com

Contents

Acknowledgements   6

Introduction   7

Making Pastry   13

Roman Origins and British Tart Baking Before 1700   19
  Savoury   20
  Sweet   33

Eighteenth- and Nineteenth-century Tarts   60
  Savoury   62
  Sweet   74

Twentieth-century Tarts   98
  Savoury   99
  Sweet   103

Afterword   124

Bibliography   125

Index   127

ACKNOWLEDGEMENTS

This book began as a germ of an idea some years back and, but for the support and enthusiasm of family and friends, nothing would have come of it. I am indebted to those many friends and guests who nobly tucked into tarts at every course.

I could not have maintained my enthusiasm and determination without the constant stream of ideas, torn-out recipes from dentists' waiting rooms, secondhand books from car boot sales and, in some instances, painstaking research in friends' own cookery libraries. The following were marvellous: Alison Leigh, Audrey Simpson, Pauline Hunt, Anne Kirk, Mary Berg, Rex Dawson, Bridget Bloom, Jean Savigny, Olwen Williams, Margaret Ambrose, Cecilia Wells, Diana Brittan, Sally Haworth, Rosemary Wolff, Mary Stott, Sam Hollick, Alice Percival, Liz Budd and Joan Winterkorn.

I should also like to thank those who responded so positively to my questions about old tarts: the County Records Offices of Cambridgeshire County Council, Hampshire County Council and Lancashire Council for their help in tracing the origins and menus for school tarts; Derbyshire County Council and Bakewell Library for their help in unearthing more background about the Bakewell tart; Kent County Council for their help in tracing the origins of the Canterbury pudding; the National Trust, including Paul Coleman and Keith Goodwin at Wimpole Hall; Trevor Brighton of the Bakewell and District Historical Society; Penny Thompson, Manager of Fitzbillies; Karen, Pastry Chef at Emmanuel College; the 'chef', the excellent pastry chefs Clive and Jane, and all the kitchen staff at Kings College, Cambridge; and the staff of Cambridge University Library, the Warburg Institute, the Barbican and Guildhall Libraries and Cambridge Central Library.

My agent Luigi Bonomi offered constant enthusiasm and informal but efficient advice, being positive and responsive throughout. I would have got nowhere without the staff at Headline: I thank Heather Holden-Brown for her infectious enthusiasm and vast knowledge and experience, Jo Roberts-Miller for dealing with the many queries so efficiently and patiently, Anne Sheasby for her considerable editing expertise and Don Last for his sensitive photographic interpretations.

There were some who were unfortunate enough to have borne the brunt of my enquiries and lapses in determination and without whom I do not think I could have completed this book. My particular thanks go to: Zarles Williams who, in spite of many other pressures, provided an anchor in discussing the recipes and whose help in cooking some of these tarts has left me with some amusing memories and a little more wisdom; Jane Renfrew, who allowed me free access to her library of books on food and cooking and offered constant support, friendship and advice based on her immense knowledge of the history of food; Angela Fritz who, together with Zoe and Daniel, showed unfailing enthusiasm for the book and the many tarts that were delivered to their door; my daughters, Anna and Louise, who listened to my moans, helped in cooking, testing and revising the recipes, while gently encouraging me to look on the bright side; and finally my husband, Dick, whose solid nurturing and practical help over many months made this book possible.

Written for anyone with an interest in food, whether knowledgeable, experienced or just starting out, the recipes in these pages originate from old cookery books and many other formal and informal family sources. Some have been reworked, using modern ingredients, while others have been left largely untouched. Either way, they reflect the original historical backcloth and originality of the ingredients and styles of cooking. They have been chosen for their honest simplicity, for their capacity to inspire experimentation and for their ability to put us in touch with our own memories of family, friends and good times together.

I became interested in baking tarts when, still in my early twenties, I acquired a large ready-made family of children. Baking a tart became for me a symbol for bringing people together and the beginning of some kind of shared history and I began to get requests for repeat bakings of tarts. This gave me confidence to experiment with the mixing of ingredients and ways of presenting them. This new-found boldness coincided with the gift of an old recipe book. Once this had been devoured I began more serious research, first in the Cambridge University Library, then the Warburg Institute in London (home of some of Elizabeth David's collection) and, finally, the City of London Library, home of Jane Grigson's and André Simon's collection, among others.

Every tart in this book has a history in terms of the baking and seeking out of information. This exercise has also led me to several firm conclusions, one of which is that there is no point in abstruse discussions about what is meant by a tart, as distinct from a pie, quiche, cheesecake or anything else. For me, as for most authorities I have consulted, the really distinguishing feature of a tart is that it must have some kind of pastry base. Whether or not it has a pastry lid is irrelevant.

But why is it necessary to write such a book? Isn't it easier to pick up a tart from the supermarket and save one's energy for other parts of a meal? Of course I have bought tarts and, when graced with good ice cream, a dollop of crème fraîche or a good sauce, they can be quite wonderful. But these are senses shared with many thousands of others – no piece of you, no unique flavours, nothing new, and no personal pleasure in the making and sharing. Baking an old tart is taking a step back into the richest of British cooking traditions. As the tart is placed on the table you are drawing people together to be part of the mystery that you have recreated. It is a source of curiosity and intrigue, widening our understanding and love of natural ingredients. Baking a tart makes us find time for ourselves and, in so doing, we make time for others.

Although the tart began long before the Romans, it was the Romans we have to thank for some of our earliest tart-making traditions. They specialised in flower and fruit tarts, typically including a mix of elderflower, roses, dates, cherries and pine nuts mixed together with the herb 'rue', honey and well-beaten eggs, and cooked in wine. They brought their love of such food to England. They introduced the cherry and were able to grow apricots, figs, grapes and almonds in southern England; these fruits were sometimes dried or stored in honey, syrup or alcohol, ensuring that the tart ingredients remained sweet and distinctive in flavour. The Romans were also fond of fish and seafood, fresh herbs and meats. Their cooking was a model of creativity and inventiveness, using sauces, alcohol and decoration to enrich their tarts and pies.

Wealthy households in Britain then had a rich fund of ingredients to include in a tart or pie. It was assumed that the natural ingredients of butter, milk, curd cheese, whey, cream, honey, eggs and flour would be available. Added to this were the many herbs and spices, dried and fresh fish and game. From the mix of dried or preserved fruits, nuts (almonds especially) and natural fresh and other ingredients sprang many of the very oldest tart recipes, as described in the earlier recipes in this book.

The more wealthy the household, the more frequent was the use of imported ingredients and delicacy of flavours. Thus in the fifteenth century, the royal families and other wealthy households would perhaps sup on a musk, fig and almond tart while neighbouring peasants might be enjoying a simple curd tart with a few dried raisins, a fresh pea and honey tart in early summer or a crushed rose-hip tart in autumn.

The arrival of new ingredients such as peas, asparagus, artichokes and broccoli from France, Italy and Spain, and later citrus fruits and vegetables, increased flexibility for cooks. The arrival and colonisation of fruits such as gooseberries, strawberries, raspberries and rhubarb led to a new wave of tart-making because the fruits were seen as sufficiently distinctive in flavour to resist being boiled down into a compote, which is what happened to such fruits as apples and quinces.

Almost anything could be put in a tart. Even the poorest families were familiar with the benefits of herbs and potions and so it was often the case that ingredients were mixed with a specific medicinal or ritualistic fruit – so there would be tarts to increase fertility, to fend off melancholia or to increase male potency, for example – each reflecting the known folklore about the use of herbs and spices. Here is an example from Elizabethan times:

> . . . *tart to provoke courage either in man or woman. Take a quart of good wine and boil therein two Burre roots scraped clean, two good quinces and a potato root well pared, and an ounce of Dates, and when all these are boiled verie tender, let them be drawne through a strainer wine and al, and then be put in the yolks of eight eggs, and the braines of three or fower cocke sparrows, and straine them into the other, and a little rosewater, and seeth them all with sugar, cinnamon and ginger and cloves and mace and put in a little sweet butter and set it upon a chafing dish of coales between hot platters and so let boile till it be something big.*

Tarts and pies were used to hide and embellish less appetising, dry, salted, tainted or sour ingredients, often through mixing together the savoury and sweet. Like the origins of today's mince (mynce) pies, a rich butter pastry filled with a mixture of chopped meat, spinach, herbs, spices, dried fruits and sugar, mounded together and topped with a sheet of rich pastry and, once baked, given an 'icing' of rosewater and sugar, for example.

These early tarts were more like a child's creation with some muddy-looking playdoh, with or without a bit of decoration. There were no fluted tart tins, marble rolling pins or oven thermometers; most of the tarts were crude and poorly finished raised pies, hand-sculpted flat tarts or dish tarts. Often the flour used, by the poor cooks in particular, was unrefined and the result was a strong-tasting pastry, but to counterbalance this the ingredients enjoyed an earthy robustness which I hope I have recaptured in the earlier recipes.

In wealthier households, flour was more refined and paler and there was a greater sophistication in the finished product. In Elizabethan times, the rich butter pastry was made with flour, butter, as many eggs as possible, rosewater and spices. It was repeatedly rolled with each rolling incorporating a knob of butter, just as with modern puff pastry. Sugar was sprinkled all over it and, once baked, it was eaten and enjoyed as a large, very rich and spicy shortbread biscuit. More sophisticated pastries were tried, such as the *croquant* or crackling pastry, introduced from France at the beginning of the seventeenth century; it was made of flour, sugar and egg whites, baked in rounds which then formed the base for fresh or cooked fruit – a rather free form of fruit tart. Other ingredients were used in pastry-making with herbs, almonds and, later, dried coconut being common. These and others are described in the chapter on pastry-making.

In fact, the almond has played a major role in the history of tart-making because it had so many uses. In the Middle Ages, it was a mainstay of cooks: its greatest use was in the production of almond milk (pounded almonds, sugar and water or wine) which could be used instead of milk in the making of curd and custard tarts, and as a base in which to stew certain other ingredients. It was much used for cooking both savoury and sweet ingredients and for making pies and tarts on 'fysshe' (non-meat) days. In the late Middle Ages, the invention of marzipan (ground almonds and sugar, called 'marchpane') reached us from Italy and it became a flexible and glamorous tool for pastry cooks. At great feasts, for example, it was made into elaborate, decorative 'subtleties' – exotic and spectacular marzipan sculptures placed on the table and designed to prompt praise and adulation. The almond exemplifies the uniqueness of a tart which, by slowly releasing the combined flavours during cooking, transforms something mundane into something magical – no wonder that some of our best-loved recipes include an almond base.

Because a tart was not just a straightforward compilation of ingredients but more a work of art, the key to success lay in the ingenuity and skill, first as a gatherer of ingredients and then in knowing how to mix them. The fact that even the poorest housewife had access to fields, hedgerows and rich people's back gardens is clear when looking at old recipes. It was taken for granted that, where possible, a cook would include the chopped or pounded leaves of herbs such as sorrel, lovage, tansy and fennel, or flowers – roses, marigolds, cowslips and primroses. She would certainly be making her own rosewater as opposed to using suspect well water and she would be very able to produce candied flowers such as violets with which to decorate or help fill her tarts. Her knowledge of the hedgerows gave her ready access to mushrooms and toadstools, to rosehips, elderflowers and berries, hawthorn, crabapples and cobnuts.

The storecupboard yielded a constant supply of such items as stale bread and cake, rice and, in some cases, dried fruits, herbs and spices, jellies and syrups and jars of honey (marmalade and jams came later) and, if a cow were at her disposal, milk, cream and butter were readily available. Without the use of measuring jugs, sophisticated ovens or any written advice on quantities, the skill lay in getting the right mix of ingredients and a simple medium in which to mix them – melted butter, alcohol, cream, almond milk and cheese.

Colour was also a part of the act of transforming the dull into something interesting, and contrasting colours were sought either within one tart or through a number of different coloured tarts. Ordinary beige pastry was made golden yellow with the addition of saffron. Even savoury tarts were made more colourful with marigold, primrose and cowslips. Sweet yellow tarts were made from the egg yolks and white tarts from the whites. Fruits were chosen not just for their taste but for their capacity after long boiling to produce different coloured 'tart stuff'. This boiling would quite likely be done in alcohol which would enhance the end colour. Prunes cooked in dark red wine produced 'black' tarts; raspberries cooked in a light rosé a rich red; and unseeded grapes cooked in white wine an olive green.

This desire to produce something colourful reflected the fact that the tart would be placed ceremoniously alongside other major dishes such as roasted boar's head and it had to look good. Certainly, when a group of friends and I reproduced a seventeenth-century meal in a Cambridge College, the pyramid of coloured tarts was an unusual centrepiece. The drive for impact in presentation even led to the cooks insisting on using only copper saucepans so that the copper would colour their grapes (and their vegetables) bright green. The well-known northern Harlequin Tart (see page 76) with different coloured segments of lemon curd, greengage jam, marmalade, raspberry jam and blackcurrant jam is a legacy from the era of the 'colourful tart stuff'.

For many early cooks, the lack of access to any oven with any degree of sophistication, or in many instances any oven at all, meant that there was an element of uncertainty and luck in determining the end product. In some cases, poorer families relied on squeezing their pies and puddings into the town or village bakery's ovens either before or after the bread was done. In order to recognise their tart it was necessary to decorate it in a distinctive fashion, rather like the branding of sheep on the hills, and some of these decorative twists and twirls have survived until now. The end product might be mis-shapen and ash-covered but it was prized by all who ate it.

Like everything else, the history of tart-making shows how susceptible we have been to different trends and influences and how we in our turn have influenced cooking abroad. There were food fashions which in many ways were more short-lived and hyped even than those of today for they were at the mercy of major new arrivals. The excitement which greeted the arrival of sugar (in crude loaf form to begin with), the first bananas (seventeenth century), chocolate (eighteenth century) and coffee, the tomato (or 'love apple'), broccoli, peas, beans syrup and the accidental discovery of treacle (nineteenth century) represent key moments in the history of tart-making. Often the fashions were based on rumour: the fear of fresh fruit – it being thought of as a spreader of diseases, including the plague – led to the preference for cooked fruit tarts. The temporary unpopularity of egg whites in the eighteenth century (thought to induce cold body temperatures) led for some time to a dearth of meringue toppings and decoration.

Our influence abroad is most apparent when looking at the spread of British cooking in America, beginning with the pilgrims in the seventeenth century taking with them a store of ingredients and 'recipes' which soon became adapted to the new surroundings and fresh ingredients. The tradition of pie-making sprang from Britain and the modern versions of the recipes reflect those earlier British origins. Our capacity to export comfort food in the form of cherry, apple, buttermilk and pumpkin pies was a major contribution to American homeliness.

We have adapted some of our recipes to those of other countries and, for a time, the great rivalry between French and British cooks and chefs (at its height in the seventeenth century) led to frequent borrowing of each other's ideas. The interesting difference between the two is that most French cooking, writing and tart-making was undertaken by men, whereas in Britain it was the women who were shaping developments with their unpretentious and popular books for other female cooks. And it is this genuine 'British housewife as tart-maker' that I have tried to capture in this book.

In Victorian times, there was a greater melding of country baking tradition with some more urban ingredients, helped by better transport and communications. The tradition of eating in style and in large quantities had spread to a greater number of people. Train travel encouraged the use of the picnic hamper and the Victorian picnic gave rise to innumerable cooking rituals, one of which was the inclusion of baked pies and tarts, adding to the versatility and range of small- and large-scale cooks. It was always thought prudent to take 'one old lady' on a picnic, largely because she would be proficient in packing and unpacking the pies and tarts from the picnic hamper.

The influence of the major wars in the twentieth century produced what we now think of as the austerity pies and tarts, some of which are enjoying a minor comeback – Lord Woolton Pie (see page 102) is one example – others made do with whatever was to hand, using up shrivelled and mean titbits and processed imports, such as corned beef and spam, hoping to transform them by wrapping them in pastry.

But there are many regional and seasonal traditions which have outlasted all wars and fashions and which are celebrated in this book. The Huntingdon Fidget Pie (see page 62), with bacon and apples, and the Welsh Leek, Bacon and Goat's Cheese Tart (see page 100) are examples. As well as the truly old English custard, curd and fruit tarts, there are many real old favourites from our childhoods – those cooked by our grandmothers, by our school cooks and by many a member of the Women's Institute. For trusted and tried tarts I have included alternative recipes, hoping to strike a chord with as many readers as possible. For example, in trying to find the genuine and definitive version of the Bakewell Tart I tried more than twenty recipes, each one of them being thought of as the original and definitive tart handed down from the days of Jane Austen. I have tried to distil the baking experience so that the recipes used in this book are true to the original, while at the same time having the failsafe capacity to succeed. Where necessary I've adapted ingredients, often because the end taste is better. But there is no tart in this book that is not steeped in history and that will not encourage you to delve deeper and to experiment further.

For me there is a particular nostalgia attached to the Britishness of cooking, mirrored in my family upbringing during the 1950s and 60s. This was a time when women were confined to the home and where they were forced, through a lack of servants, to undertake cooking from a limited knowledge base. The books of the time recapture the need to pass on to others newly acquired skills such as pastry-making in easy step-by-step guides, in order that well-groomed and freshly pinafored housewives could produce a constant supply of tempting puddings, cakes and tarts for their hungry, bread-winning husbands. The result was an energy directed at the mastering of timeless cooking traditions and a deference to previous generations. An injection of new life was provided by the writings of Elizabeth David, Jane Grigson and others who sought to enliven British cooking with the use of colourful Mediterranean, Middle Eastern and Asian ingredients. The rediscovery of the courgette and coriander are typical of this new wave of cooking.

Another underlying theme in this book is the timeless quality of good British ingredients, whether from hedgerows, back gardens, allotments or orchards, and the knotting together of these with the many centuries of traditions that have accompanied their use. Although the underlying principle of tart-making is the unhurried pleasure to be had from the slow passage through the different cooking stages – from the loving accumulation of the ingredients, through the gentle art of mixing and rolling the pastry, and the patient wait for the ingredients to meld and send out their delicious aromas – this book nevertheless recognises the need for many of us to achieve the same results quickly.

The message I am keen to get over here is that these tart recipes should be used as a starting point for your own experimentation and creativity. It won't matter, for example, if you use one spice rather than another, if you use dried biscuit or cake crumbs rather than breadcrumbs, or if you substitute sugar for honey. These are old recipes which have been brought up to date; and sometimes a number of different versions have been merged into one in order to capture the key features of many centuries of British tarts, while at the same time adapting them to suit the tastes of today.

The idea is for each of these old tarts to be a unique creation, one which is steeped in longstanding British cooking traditions, but whose construction has been made quite simple and may indeed be very modern. Many of the first tarts were primitive, but homely and inviting; others were splendid, grandiose works of art. I hope you will feel that this book encourages you to produce old tarts which reflect you, your history and your creativity and which give you enormous pleasure.

Tracing the history of tarts and tart-making offers a window into the intriguing and sometimes contentious world of pastry-making. Ideas and hints abound in books and magazines but all too often these 'how to' sections simply add to the lurking sense of inadequacy that dogs so many budding cooks. Many households today never see a homemade tart, pie or pastry because the cook of the house 'never cooks pastry – it is too difficult'. I hear this phrase often, even from otherwise very competent cooks. I think this is a great pity, as there is no mystique about the making of pastry, and not to make it means the denial of some of our most memorable, interesting and delicious traditional dishes. Pastry in a tart should be like a good accompanist to a singer – a key component but never stealing the show.

For those readers who are already established pastry-makers with a sound track record in tart-making, your interest in this book will be in the more unusual tart fillings. You will not need to read the following few paragraphs on making pastry as you will already have your own well-tried methods and formulae and many of you will no doubt be addicted to the food processor.

This section does not aim to be comprehensive or prescriptive. It is a simple account of what I have found works for me and is no more than a simple exposition of my own feelings and philosophy about the making of pastry. I hope to encourage someone starting pastry cooking to 'have a go' – to forget about having all the right experience and equipment and to put inhibitions and inadequacies to one side. Making a tart is a work of art, born of contentment and pleasure, and each step involves a unique creative journey. The first step in this journey is, and must be, making the pastry.

When I first began making tarts my energy was focused solely on getting the tart fillings right. As a result, I was only too happy to use good ready-made fresh pastry. This helped me to take the plunge, to relax and feel free to experiment. Nowadays, I almost always make my own pastry, usually in batches. I have no idea whether I have 'pastry hands' – light or cool fingers known as 'tour de main' in France – but I know I love blending fat into flour. I also love the discipline that comes from the various stages in tart-making.

However, I still occasionally use good fresh pastry from supermarkets – especially if I am in a real hurry or trying out a new filling. And I do think that those nervous about pastry-making should consider beginning their creative journey by using ready-made pastry, enabling someone new to tart-making to embark upon and enjoy cooking the unusual and delicious recipes in this book. And if using ready-made pastry enables an inexperienced cook to 'get into' pastry-making, then he or she might soon want to tackle it from scratch. Making your own pastry is perhaps the most therapeutic and enjoyable form of cooking.

EQUIPMENT

Those who shy away from pastry-making often use the excuse of poor equipment and lack of knowledge about what to buy. But to cook the tarts in this book you need very little equipment.

TART TINS

A source of terror and panic for many. For most, but not all, of the tarts in this book, I use only two types of metal tins: (i) a shallow 23cm/9 in (about 2.5cm/1 in deep) round tart tin, to be found in any supermarket; and (ii) a deep 23cm/9 in (about 4cm/1½ in deep) round tin, now beginning to appear in supermarkets and easily available in most cook shops.

Both of these types of tins have serrated, curvy edges and may be referred to as quiche or flan tins. You can also get them with straight edges.

However, you can use any other shape or size of tin and you will find that I use square or oblong tins in one or two cases. You will want to browse through stores and experiment with different tins. The only thing you have to be careful about is the volume of the tin – you must adjust the amounts of ingredients accordingly.

TARTLET TINS

These are available in most cook shops. The best size to get a reasonable idea of what the full tart tastes like is the 8cm (3¼ in) round tin which is commonly used for savoury or sweet tartlets. With a few on hand you can use up any spare pastry and/or filling.

METAL BAKING SHEETS

These are invaluable. They can be placed in the oven while it is heating up to the required temperature and so provide a hot sheet on which to place the pastry shell, thereby helping to avoid soggy bottoms. They can also be used to help transport uncooked tarts with super-wobbly fillings to the oven. They are available in many supermarkets or cook shops.

It is worth getting the non-stick variety if you can or, even better, the slightly more expensive ones with good heat-conducting qualities. These sheets can also be used to bake free-form, unstructured tarts, like the rustic Rhubarb and Strawberry Tart cooked in Beer described in this book (see page 90–1). All you do is fold the pastry around the filling. They are great confidence boosters.

WIRE RACK

On which a cooked tart can cool.

LARGE BOWL

A really attractive, and loved, large bowl. In this you can do all your rubbing and mixing. Your heart should lift every time you see it.

PLATE

A loved, large old plate on which to place your tart with pride.

All other equipment is really a luxury and I suppose one could argue that it adds to the creative process if you have to make do and invent your own substitutes for items such as rolling pins (empty wine bottles) and baking beans (uncooked rice or beans), although there is no greater pleasure than acquiring and using favourite pieces of cooking equipment.

PLAIN SHORTCRUST PASTRY

225g (8 oz) plain flour
1 large pinch of salt
115g (4 oz) good quality unsalted butter
   (or 55g/2 oz unsalted butter and
   55g/2 oz lard), chopped
a small amount of very cold water

Sift the flour from quite a height into a bowl, allowing lots of air in. Add salt, then rub the chopped butter into the flour using the tips of your fingers only, until the mixture becomes like breadcrumbs; use your fingers repeatedly to lift the mixture up, so as to let in as much air as possible.

Sprinkle cold water over the mixture, then use a flat-sided palette knife or similar to bring it together so that it just starts to leave the sides of the bowl. Knead very briefly with your fingers into the shape of a ball. Wrap in clingfilm, polythene or foil and put in the fridge to rest for 30 minutes. While the pastry is resting you can prepare the filling. Take the pastry from the fridge and, using a rolling pin, roll it out on a lightly floured surface, rolling away from you, until the pastry is about 3mm (⅛ in) thick.

Line the tart tin – this is done most easily by rolling the pastry around the rolling pin and then carefully unrolling it over the tin. Push the pastry right up to the edge and make sure that it reaches the top of the tin's rim. The lined tin should then be returned to the fridge for a further 30 minutes before being put in the oven; this will prevent the tart from shrinking too much during cooking.

RICH SWEET SHORTCRUST PASTRY (PÂTE BRISÉE)

225g (8 oz) plain flour
1 large pinch of salt (even though this is
   a sweet pastry)
115g (4 oz) butter
55g (2 oz) caster sugar or sifted icing
   sugar
1 egg yolk
2 tablespoons very cold water

Mix the flour, salt and butter as above. When the butter is mixed in, add the sugar and then make a well in the centre. Add the egg yolk to the well and sprinkle the flour with the cold water.

Use a flat-sided knife to bring the flour over the egg yolk and to take in the water. Shape into a ball and rest and roll out the pastry as before.

Some think that a few drops of vanilla essence enhance this pastry, particularly when the filling is a cooked custard or a 'cheese'. Add the vanilla essence with the egg yolk.

Two Types of Pastry for Tarts

I have stuck here to the very simplest of pastries – a plain shortcrust pastry for use with both sweet and savoury tarts, and a rich sweet shortcrust pastry for use only with sweet tarts. For those who are experienced pastry-makers, using richer pastry bases such as pâte sucrée would enhance the recipes for sweet tarts in many instances. It is also possible to achieve a more authentic old pastry base by mixing wholemeal and self-raising flour together. There are, too, flours available in wholefood shops which mirror those of earlier centuries – Marriages Flour is just one example.

Note: The quantities are sufficient for most of the tarts in this book – 225g (8 oz) – but I suggest that if you intend cooking a number of tarts then you should consider doubling the quantities and put half away in the fridge (where it will keep, wrapped, for 3 days) or in a freezer (where it will keep for 3 months).

Mixing with the Food Processor

It is only realistic to accept that many of us will depend to a greater or lesser extent on the food processor when making our tarts.

To make the pastry, combine the flour, salt and butter in the processor. Mix for 10–12 seconds. Add the water and mix for a further 10–12 pulses until the mixture holds together, but before it turns into a ball (if it is processed for too long it will become tough). If it is too dry, add a little more water and pulse 2 or 3 more times.

Wrap the pastry in clingfilm, polythene or foil and transfer to the fridge. Rest and roll out the pastry as on page 15.

Pre-Baking and Baking 'Blind'

Having lined your tart tin with pastry, and after a further rest in the fridge, the next step is critical for avoiding something that can spoil any tart – a soggy bottom. Most pastry cooks have their own ideas on how to avoid soggy bottoms, but there are two main ways:

Baking 'blind' – I am addicted to my original 1960s Elizabeth David clay baking beans, and am a great believer in baking 'blind'. Line the pastry case with non-stick baking paper or greaseproof paper and fill with baking beans. Place on a pre-heated baking sheet and bake in a pre-heated hot oven (200ºC/400ºF/Gas 6) for 15 minutes. Remove from the oven and lift the beans out with the paper. Prick the pastry base all over using a fork and brush with beaten egg before returning it to the oven for a further 5–10 minutes, until it turns a light golden brown.

Pre-baking – prick the uncooked pastry shell thoroughly with a fork to release some of the trapped air, brush the base with beaten egg to provide a waterproof coating (you can also use a sweet glaze such as warm, sieved apricot jam) and then cook in a warm oven (180ºC/350ºF/Gas 4) for 25 minutes, preferably on a pre-heated baking sheet. This method works perfectly and it has the advantage of involving only one instead of two procedures. I miss my beans, but I am recommending using this second method in this book.

After the Tart is Cooked

Unless you feel super confident, I suggest you leave the tart as it is in the tin to cool down.

If it is to be eaten at room temperature, or colder, then you can ease it from the edges of the tin using a palette knife and let it cool down until you feel it is solid enough for you to remove the metal plate. Then put it on a wire rack to cool.

OLD-WORLD PASTRY

Most old tarts were baked with a flaky or puff-pastry base but I find that shortcrust pastry works better and is less rich and cloying. There are ways of making the pastry taste of the past, complementing the fillings and adding to the overall impact and appearance. Certainly there is no more welcoming smell than cinnamon pastry cooking in the oven. Here are a few suggestions for giving your pastry the old-world feel. In all cases add the suggested ingredients to the flour *before* mixing:

FOR ORANGE, LEMON, APPLE AND MINCEMEAT TARTS – add a tablespoon of finely grated lemon or orange zest and a few drops of orange flower essence if available.

FOR ALL OLD CUSTARD, ALMOND OR HONEY TARTS – add 1 teaspoon of ground cinnamon or grated nutmeg, or a few drops of vanilla or almond essence.

FOR ALMOND TARTS – use chopped amaretti biscuits or ground almonds instead of some of the flour.

FOR (NON-MEAT) SAVOURY TARTS – add 1 tablespoon of chopped fresh mixed herbs.

FOR CHEESE AND HERB TARTS – add any chopped nuts instead of some of the flour.

FOR EGG, HAM OR BACON TARTS – mix 1 large tablespoon of wholegrain mustard with the flour or ½ teaspoon of dried mustard powder.

FOR ROUGH OLD TARTS – blend in 1 tablespoon of oatmeal or use the oatmeal when rolling out the pastry.

GLAZING AND DECORATING

Old tarts are renowned for their colour and decoration. Many were very simple and involved brushing with beaten egg, egg white or egg yolk. For sweet tarts, different spices and sugars would also be added, resulting in an attractive sweet crust. Simpler still is the habit of just sprinkling spices or herbs on an unglazed surface prior to cooking, or when the cooked tart is placed on the table.

For fruit tarts, a simple glaze is provided by melting redcurrant jelly (or jelly made from other red fruits), apricot jam or honey. Most sweet tarts, when brought to the table, look better for a sprinkling of sifted icing sugar or, even better, a liberal sprinkling of sugar which has been caramelised under a hot grill, though this practice has its detractors.

I have not mentioned fancy decorations, such as edgings, as the whole point of this book is to produce earthy, homely looking tarts as if plucked from a medieval bread oven. On the other hand, the lattice effect resulting from making a pattern on the surface of the tart – often from strips of leftover pastry – is worth having, especially for fruit tarts such as cherry or gooseberry, which produce a lot of juice. The lattice looks even better if the pastry strips are brushed with beaten egg.

Icing is normally associated with cakes, but the look of some tarts can be transformed by giving a simple coating or drizzling of thin water or glacé icing, sometimes enhanced with a little lemon juice, orange flower water or rosewater.

Extra Hints for Making Pastry

1 Plan to enjoy it, put on your favourite music and remember that a glass of chilled wine helps to keep your hands cold.

2 Never let anything get warm before it goes in the oven. Keep everything as cold as possible.

3 The oven must be at the required temperature when you place the pastry shell on the metal baking sheet which has been heating up with the oven. This means that you turn on the oven to reach the required temperature well before you start making the pastry.

4 Think of creating a pastry shell with 3mm ($\frac{1}{8}$ in) thickness of pastry (for tartlets it should be less).

5 Lightly greasing the tart tin with a little butter before lining it with pastry and placing it in the fridge will assist you when it comes to removing the cooked tart from the tin.

6 Always check that you have included the salt.

7 If you are apprehensive about the tart you are cooking, perhaps for a special occasion, reassure yourself by cooking a tartlet at the same time. You can then sample the tart in advance.

8 If the pastry edges are in danger of getting too brown, cover with a strip of crinkled foil. This can be a particular problem with tartlets.

9 The tarts in this book are designed for immediate or almost immediate consumption (within 24 hours). Most of them can be frozen and you may find that you will enjoy tart-making even more when you have longer sessions yielding a freezer's worth in one go. But the great strength of a tart is that you can make it several hours before the meal, thus taking much of the pressure off cooking at the last minute.

*T*he tarts in this section provide an introduction to tart-making from Roman times, through the Middle Ages and up to the seventeenth century. The examples chosen are typical of this period and between them they exhibit some of the principal characteristics of tart-cooking dating back more than 1,500 years.

The first and startling impression of Roman cookery is its sophistication, in its range of ingredients, in the unusual mix of herbs and spices, in their cooking technology and use of equipment – the Romans were very knowledgeable about ovens – and in the evident desire to please and impress. The tarts emanating from this time reflect their 'passions' – their love of seafood, their interest in fresh fruit and vegetables and their ability to mix the sweet, sour and even the pungent to enhance the principal ingredients.

Cooking in medieval Britain and up to the end of the seventeenth century was, by comparison, simple and unfussy, relying on fewer ingredients but still with a love of spices and a capacity to mingle sweet and savoury. It was during this period, too, that many ingredients made their first appearance in Britain, particularly following the great voyages of discovery in the sixteenth and seventeenth centuries. There are recurrent ingredients including almonds, custards, honey, curds and spices; and the tarts made from such ingredients are distinctive in their delicacy of flavour and versatility of use. Other ingredients introduced during this period become second nature by the end of the book – almond milk, verjuice (the juice of unripe fruits), saffron, cinnamon, nutmeg, ginger, rose and orange waters.

The tarts in this section also introduce one of the most consistent features of pastry-making and tart-baking in Britain – the determination to make the finished product as colourful and appetising as circumstances allow. The use of marigold flowers to colour the curd cheese tart, the decoration of the humblest pastry using sprinkled spices, herbs or icing made with egg white and sugar – both confirm the truth that baking, perhaps more than any other cooking activity, reveals a supreme attempt to give of oneself so as to give pleasure. Yet the presentation of the tarts was characterised by simplicity. The cooks of the day were as inventive as they had ever been, glazing and decorating their tarts in often very imaginative ways but, with a limited range of ingredients and access to only the simplest of cooking technology, cooks were rarely pretentious. Their methodology was confined to very basic techniques and cooking was done in crude and often wholly unreliable ovens.

Roman Seafood Tart

SERVES 4–6

175g (6 oz) plain shortcrust pastry
(see page 15)

55g (2 oz) unsalted butter

550g (1¼ lb) prepared (shelled, peeled,
etc.) mixed seafood, according to
availability and taste (prawns,
scallops, crab, oysters, etc.)

3 cloves garlic, finely chopped

2 tablespoons fresh coriander, chopped

1 tablespoon fresh parsley, chopped

large pinch each of grated nutmeg
and ground ginger

1 teaspoon anchovy essence (or 1
tablespoon fish or soy sauce)

juice of ½ lemon

1 egg, plus 1 egg yolk

300ml (½ pint) double cream

salt and freshly ground black pepper

The Romans simply loved seafood. Archaeological finds in Britain and throughout the Roman Empire have uncovered pile upon pile of oyster shells and the remains of most of the seafood we normally associate with the Mediterranean. Wonderfully tempting appetisers of clams and sea urchins would be served to the Roman emperors. Although much of the seafood was eaten in a raw or fresh condition, when cooking prawns, crabs, scallops or oysters, use would often be made of the distinctive Roman 'garum' – fish sauce made from anchovy, pounded and mixed together with the fermented liquid from the entrails of salted fish. This sauce was widely used and valued for its ability to enhance the flavour of other ingredients. Unfortunately, it is no longer in production, but to recapture the garum effect, I suggest you use either anchovy essence, soy sauce or a South-east Asian fish sauce. The herbs used in this recipe are those that were available in Roman times, but you can alter these to suit your own taste.

Line a shallow 23cm (9 in) tart tin with the pastry and pre-bake or bake blind as directed on page 16. Pre-heat the oven to 190°C/375°F/Gas 5.

Heat the butter in a heavy-bottomed frying pan and add all the seafood, together with the garlic. Fry for 3–4 minutes until the fish seems cooked and the garlic is well mixed in, stirring occasionally. Add the herbs, nutmeg, ginger, anchovy essence (or fish or soy sauce) and lemon juice. Mix well, then place in the pre-baked pastry case.

In a bowl, gently beat the egg and egg yolk together. Add the cream, a little salt and some black pepper and mix well. Pour the mixture evenly over the seafood mixture. If you are using oysters, these can be placed evenly on top of the tart and then sprinkled with any remaining chopped herbs. Bake in the oven for 25 minutes or until lightly set and golden brown.

SERVE warm or cold with a watercress or rocket salad, small boiled potatoes and a wedge of lemon.

COOK'S TIP — This tart will serve 8–10 as a starter. Fennel can be substituted for the coriander.

Scottish Smoked Salmon and Cucumber Cream Cheese Tart

SERVES 4–6

175g (6 oz) plain shortcrust pastry
(see page 15)

1 large cucumber, skinned and chopped

salt and freshly ground black pepper

225g (8 oz) smoked salmon, broken
into largish pieces

225g (8 oz) cream cheese

2 eggs, plus 1 egg yolk

150ml (¼ pint) double cream

2 tablespoons finely chopped fresh
chives

2 tablespoons finely chopped fresh dill

finely grated zest and juice of 1 lemon

fresh herb sprigs, to garnish

Scotland has a long tradition of smoking both haddock and salmon. In medieval times, special smokehouses – small narrow buildings with wooden beams – dotted the countryside, although in Scotland's fishing districts, it was common for fishermen's wives to smoke their fish in their own chimneys, using peat as a fuel instead of the oak and ash preferred further south. The addition of cooked cucumber revives a tradition dating back to the sixteenth century, when English cucumbers were regarded, like courgettes, as prime targets for stuffing and baking, as well as pickling (gherkins). They have an age-old affinity with salmon.

Long regarded as a luxury food and a Christmas treat, smoked salmon is now enjoying all-year-round popularity and this tart is guaranteed not to fail.

Line a shallow 23cm (9 in) tart tin with the pastry and pre-bake or bake blind as directed on page 16. Pre-heat the oven to 200°C/400°F/Gas 6.

To salt the cucumber, put the chopped pieces in a colander and sprinkle lightly with salt. Put a small plate and a heavy object or two on top of the plate. Leave for 30 minutes, when much of the superfluous water will have drained away. Rinse, drain and dry in kitchen paper. Place the cucumber pieces, together with the smoked salmon, into the pre-baked pastry case. Set aside.

Put the cream cheese, eggs, egg yolk, cream, herbs and lemon zest and juice in a bowl with salt and pepper to taste and whisk together until well mixed. Spoon the cheese mixture over the salmon and cucumber in the pastry case. Bake in the oven for 30 minutes, or until the tart is cooked but not too dry. Garnish with fresh herb sprigs.

SERVE warm with small boiled potatoes and a green vegetable; or cold with a cucumber salad (made with sliced cucumber, lemon juice, sea salt and black pepper) or a green salad.

COOK'S TIP – This tart will serve 8–10 as a starter.

Anchovy and Sorrel Tart

SERVES 4–6

175g (6 oz) plain shortcrust pastry
(see page 15)

350g (12 oz) sorrel (or spinach and the
juice of ½ lemon, if no sorrel), stalks
removed

25g (1 oz) butter

2 tablespoons olive oil

3 onions, thinly sliced

10–12 anchovy fillets, chopped

¼ teaspoon ground cinnamon

freshly ground black pepper

2 eggs. plus 2 egg yolks

350ml (12 fl oz) double cream

In the sixteenth century, the Church appointed certain days of the year to be 'fysshe dayes' – days on which everyone was encouraged to eat fish rather than meat. This was done partly for economic reasons – to encourage the growth of shipbuilding and the marine trade – and to ensure that the country did not run out of meat. Much of the fish that was eaten was salted fish, including anchovies, that kept and travelled well. The anchovies came largely from the Mediterranean and were kept in brine.

Sorrel, listed as a herb in the thirteenth century, was originally used as a mainstay of salads, soups, tarts and sauces, but, although it grows wild throughout much of Britain, it has largely been forgotten. This is a very traditional tart and, for those who can get hold of sorrel, it is very easy to make.

Line a shallow 23cm (9 in) tart tin with the pastry and pre-bake or bake blind as directed on pages 16. Pre-heat the oven to 200°C/400°F/Gas 6.

Wash the sorrel (or spinach) and put in a pan with a little water. Put the lid on and let the sorrel simmer over the lowest possible heat for 10 minutes. Drain it in a colander, using a saucer to squeeze out as much liquid as possible. Set aside.

Melt the butter and oil in a frying pan and gently fry the onions for about 20 minutes or until they are soft and beginning to caramelise, stirring occasionally. Remove the pan from the heat and stir in the drained sorrel, anchovies, cinnamon and black pepper.

In a large bowl, beat the eggs, egg yolks and cream together, then add the sorrel mixture to the egg mixture and give it a really good stir. Pile the mixture into the pre-baked pastry case and bake in the oven for 25–30 minutes or until the filling looks set and the edges are going golden brown. Remove the tart from the oven and allow it to cool before serving.

SERVE cold with a home-made sorrel sauce – simply grind down some fresh leaves with vinegar (or wine) and sugar. Otherwise, it is very good with a tomato salad and, of course, the salt of the anchovy seems to suggest a glass of good chilled white wine.

COOK'S TIP – This tart will serve 8–10 as a starter.

Salmon and Herb Tart

SERVES 6–8

225g (8 oz) plain shortcrust pastry
  (see page 15)
675g (1½ lb) boneless salmon fillets
3 tablespoons finely chopped fresh
  parsley plus extra to garnish
3 tablespoons finely chopped fresh dill
3 tablespoons finely chopped fresh
  tarragon
55g (2 oz) butter
2 tablespoons olive oil
4 large cloves garlic, finely chopped
juice of 1 lemon
¼ teaspoon grated nutmeg
¼ teaspoon ground cinnamon
salt and freshly ground black pepper
2 eggs, plus 2 egg yolks
425ml (¾ pint) double cream

Those who bemoan the ready availability of salmon should have sympathy with the northern medieval peasant apprentices, who were so fed up with it that they pleaded for no more than three free meals of salmon a week. Salmon and other river, pond and sea fish were very common in both wealthy and poor households and the rivers of England and Scotland kept many families in food.

In medieval times, dried and fresh fruit, together with milk and strong spices, would often be included in a fish tart, and this recipe includes a medley of appropriate herbs but with fewer spices than in the past. Its origins are firmly in the Middle Ages when it would have been served up regularly to wealthy households during Lent and other 'fysshe dayes'. This is a truly scrumptious tart – so easy and versatile and yet exotic too. Leave out one of the herbs or change the balance of herbs to suit your own taste.

Line a deep 23cm (9 in) tart tin with the pastry and pre-bake or bake blind as directed on page 16. Pre-heat the oven to 190°C/375°F/Gas 5.

Chop the salmon into small chunks or flakes. Put all the herbs in a large bowl and add the salmon, pressing the herbs into the salmon flesh until the chunks are as green as possible.

Heat the butter and oil in a heavy-bottomed pan. Add the garlic and fry very gently for no more than 1 minute. Add the salmon chunks and fry them very quickly, turning them over so that the skin turns pale but the insides are still dark pink. Add the lemon juice, sprinkle with nutmeg and cinnamon and season with salt and pepper. Lift it all out of the pan with a slotted spoon and place in the pre-baked pastry case.

Using the same bowl, with its remnants of herbs etc, mix together the eggs, egg yolks, cream and salt and pepper to taste. Pour into the pastry case. Bake in the oven for 35–40 minutes and then test to see whether the mixture has set; if not, bake for a further 5 minutes. When ready, allow to cool a little and garnish with a little chopped parsley.

SERVE warm with new potatoes, a green vegetable and a wedge of lemon, or cold with a green salad.

COOK'S TIP – This tart can be baked in six 14cm (5½ in) tartlets tins. Reduce the cooking time to about 20 minutes.

A Medieval Tart of Brie

SERVES 4–6

175g (6 oz) plain shortcrust pastry
(see page 15)

115g (4 oz) Brie (weighed without rind)

425ml (¾ pint) double cream

1 teaspoon saffron strands

½ teaspoon ground mace or nutmeg

1 teaspoon light soft brown sugar

salt and freshly ground black pepper

3 eggs, plus 2 egg yolks

*M*uch food and drink that was introduced into wealthier households in medieval Britain emanated from France and because transport was slower than today a product that ripened slowly was ideal. Brie, made from cow's milk, was being written about as long ago as the eighth century and originated in Meaux, east of Paris; it was then preferred in its fresh, as opposed to its ripened, condition. Because Brie can be used to define any cheese with a similar processing history, there are on record locally produced British Brie cheeses dating from the time of the Norman Conquest. Cheese tart was a favourite with wealthier households throughout the Middle Ages and simple versions involved breaking up the cheese and mixing it with butter and egg yolks.

The tart I describe here is richer and more interesting than many other cheese tarts and makes an easy and delicious centrepiece for all types of salad and green vegetable accompaniments.

Line a shallow 23cm (9 in) tart tin with the pastry and pre-bake or bake blind as directed on page 16. Pre-heat the oven to 220°C/425°F/Gas 7.

Chop the cheese into small chunks and place in a small oven-proof bowl and cover with half the cream. Put the Brie and cream into the oven for 10 minutes to melt. Remove from the oven and reduce the oven temperature to 180°C/350°F/Gas 4.

Meanwhile, warm the remaining cream in a pan, remove from the heat, add the saffron and leave to infuse for a few minutes. Place the melted Brie and cream in a food processor and blend until well mixed. Pour into a bowl and add the saffron, cream, mace or nutmeg, sugar and salt and pepper.

In a separate large bowl, lightly beat the eggs and egg yolks, add the cream/cheese mixture and mix well, making sure the eggs and cream are well blended. Pour into the pre-baked pastry case and bake in the oven for 30 minutes or until the filling is set and has risen up in a puffy golden splendour.

SERVE warm or cold with a mixed green or tomato salad.

Lovage, Tomato and Cheese Tart

SERVES 4–6

175g (6 oz) plain shortcrust pastry
(see page 15)
25g (1 oz) unsalted butter
2 tablespoons olive oil
2 onions, finely chopped
3 cloves garlic, finely chopped
1 tablespoon finely chopped fresh
lovage (only the young green leaves)
or 4 small stalks celery, finely chopped
3 eggs
300ml (½ pint) double cream
salt and freshly ground black pepper
4 ripe tomatoes, skinned and finely
chopped (throw away excess liquid)
115g (4 oz) mature Cheddar cheese, grated

ovage is a herb with a long culinary history. It was much used by the Romans and has inspired many a cook to plan his meals long before he needed to. A famous Roman saying was 'first pound pepper and lovage', rather like the Elizabethan cook's saying 'first take six swans', and lovage appears in many old Roman recipes. As its name indicates, lovage was often used in classical and medieval times as a love potion but was also used as a common and valued cooking ingredient.

Lovage is used much less today, although it is an attractive and easy herb to grow. It has a distinctive and strong taste, so you don't need much of it, and it can be used in the same way as celery. If, as is likely, you do not have a clump of young lovage in your herb garden, and can't get hold of any, then use celery (but you will need to use a slightly larger amount of celery and cook the tart for a little longer).

Line a shallow 23cm (9 in) tart tin with the pastry and pre-bake or bake blind as directed on page 16. Pre-heat the oven to 190°C/375°F/Gas 5.

Melt the butter and olive oil in a heavy-bottomed frying pan. Add the onion and garlic and fry for 2 minutes, stirring. Turn the heat down to very low, put the lid on and gently cook for up to 10 minutes or until the onion is soft and beginning to look golden, stirring occasionally. Add the lovage and stir for 1 minute (if you are using celery, replace the lid and cook on the very low heat for a further 5 minutes). Remove the pan from the heat and set aside.

Put the eggs in a bowl and beat lightly. Add the cream and beat for a few seconds, then add salt and pepper to taste.

Drain as much juice from the tomatoes as possible and add them, together with the lovage mixture and three-quarters of the cheese, to the egg mixture. Stir, then spoon the mixture into the pre-baked pastry case. Sprinkle the remaining cheese over the top of the tart and bake in the oven for 30 minutes or until the cheese is bubbling brown and the filling looks set.

SERVE warm with a green salad.

Fresh Herb Tart

SERVES 4–6

175g (6 oz) plain shortcrust pastry,
   rolled out in some finely chopped
   parsley (see page 15)
25g (1 oz) butter
1 onion, thinly sliced
4 spring onions, chopped
3 cloves garlic, crushed
2 tablespoons chopped fresh parsley
2 tablespoons chopped fresh chives
2 tablespoons chopped fresh tarragon
2 tablespoons chopped fresh thyme,
   oregano or marjoram
3 eggs
225ml (8 fl oz) double cream
50ml (2 fl oz) milk
salt and freshly ground black pepper
115g (4 oz) grated Cheddar cheese

This really delicious fresh herb tart is a modern attempt at recapturing the sumptuous mix of herbs that characterised the gardens of the fourteenth and fifteenth centuries. In those days, the herb garden was often the only garden, and many plants, flowers and 'weeds' were primarily classified as herbs because of their many uses. Although the mix of herbs here is a modern one, the opportunity is there to use any combination. Dill would be an interesting alternative. It is one of the oldest herbs and was used by magicians in casting their spells. Parsley is used in both the pastry and filling and you can use the flat-leafed variety if that is easier to find.

Try to use only fresh herbs but dried herbs can be used as a last resort. Perhaps more than any other tart, this one illustrates how herbs can very gently release their unique aromas into the cooking.

Line a shallow 23cm (9 in) tart tin with the pastry and pre-bake or bake blind as directed on pages 16. Pre-heat the oven to 190°C/375°F/Gas 5.

Melt the butter in a frying pan, add the onion, spring onions and garlic and cook for 10 minutes or until soft, stirring occasionally. Remove the pan from the heat, stir in the herbs and allow to cool.

In a large bowl, beat the eggs very lightly, then add the cream and milk and season with salt and pepper. Add three-quarters of the cheese to the egg mixture.

Spread the onion and herb mixture in the pre-baked pastry case and cover with the egg mixture. Sprinkle the remaining cheese over the top. Bake in the oven for 20–30 minutes, or until it has a good golden brown colour.

SERVE hot or cold, on its own, with a salad, or as a substitute for potatoes or other vegetables with a main meal.

Chaucer's Sweet Garlic and Herb Tart

SERVES 4–6

175g (6 oz) plain shortcrust pastry
   (see page 15)
12 large cloves garlic (unpeeled)
2 tablespoons olive oil, for frying
2 large onions, thinly sliced
1 teaspoon light soft brown sugar
25g (1 oz) butter
2 teaspoons chopped fresh thyme
2 teaspoons chopped fresh parsley
2 teaspoons chopped fresh oregano
¼ teaspoon mace
300ml (½ pint) double cream
1 egg, plus 1 egg yolk, lightly beaten
   (just enough to mix)
salt and freshly ground black pepper

The medicinal and fortifying qualities of garlic were recognised by the Greeks and Romans but it became regarded as food for the poor – for those whose work was heavy or for those who were sick. It was shunned by the wealthy – perhaps for the obvious negative effect it had on close physical relationships. Horace, the Roman poet, thought it 'more harmful than hemlock . . . [it] could drive one's lover to refuse to kiss and to retreat to the far side of the bed'. The British, although cautious about its use, were aware of its values and Andrew Boorde, writing in the sixteenth century, states that 'it doth kyll all manner of wormes in a mans bely'.

Now that garlic haters are on the wane and garlic bread and curries are daily fare, timid cooks are willing to include more than just the odd clove. This tart is based on the reference by Chaucer to garlic in his prologue to The Canterbury Tales.

Line a shallow 23cm (9 in) tart tin with the pastry and pre-bake or bake blind as directed on page 16. Pre-heat the oven to 190°C/375°F/Gas 5 and place a baking sheet in the oven to get hot.

Put the unpeeled cloves of garlic in a pan of boiling water and boil gently for about 10 minutes, or until the garlic can easily be pierced with a fork. Drain the garlic and squeeze the insides of the cloves from their skins. Set aside.

In a heavy-bottomed frying pan, heat the olive oil, add the onion and fry gently until soft and golden, stirring occasionally. Add the sugar, cover with a lid if possible and remove the pan from the heat.

Melt the butter in a saucepan, add all the herbs and swill around for 1 minute. Transfer to a large bowl, add the garlic cloves and mash to a pulp. Add the mace, cream, egg and egg yolk, then season with salt and black pepper and mix well, making sure that the garlic and herb pulp is distributed evenly through the cream. Transfer the mixture to the pre-baked pastry case and place in the oven on the baking sheet. Bake for about 30 minutes or until golden and set.

SERVE warm or at room temperature with a mixed green leaf and goat's cheese salad.

Pea and Artichoke Tart

SERVES 6–8

225g (8 oz) plain shortcrust pastry
(see page 15)

12 fresh artichokes, cooked and peeled,
or one 400g (14 oz) can artichoke
hearts

225g (8 oz) frozen peas (preferably
petit pois), thoroughly thawed

175ml (6 fl oz) double cream

1 egg, plus 2 egg yolks, lightly beaten

1½ teaspoons chopped fresh tarragon or
½ teaspoon dried tarragon

1 tablespoon lemon juice

½ teaspoon caster sugar

salt and freshly ground black pepper

¼ whole fresh nutmeg

fresh mint sprig and grated nutmeg or
pared lemon zest, to garnish

Artichokes were a favourite vegetable of the Romans and then in the rest of Europe from the late fifteenth century onwards. It took a while to become generally accepted but once its reputation as an aphrodisiac was widespread, it became fashionable in many wealthy households. The artichoke is frost-sensitive and thrived in the sheltered walled gardens of Victorian England.

The garden pea arrived in the sixteenth century when it was boiled whole, dipped in butter and sucked from its pod. In London, there developed a tradition of peas being sold in the streets, the pea sellers moving around the streets with a large oval pot and providing peas, together with pepper, salt and vinegar, for immediate consumption. Their natural sweetness and versatility soon made them a popular ingredient in tarts.

Artichokes were sometimes combined with mashed bone marrow or lambs' brains in tarts, but peas provided a more acceptable and attractive companion. This tart is easy, delicious and looks very attractive.

Line a deep 23cm (9 in) round tart tin or a shallow 23cm (9 in) square tin with the pastry and pre-bake or bake blind as directed on page 16. Pre-heat the oven to 190°C/375°F/Gas 5.

Roughly chop up the artichoke hearts and lay them on the base of the pre-baked pastry case.

Whizz up the peas, cream, eggs, egg yolks, tarragon, lemon juice, sugar and salt and pepper in a food processor until well mixed, then pour over the top of the artichokes. Grate the fresh nutmeg on top. Bake in the oven for 30–35 minutes or until the mixture is set but still squidgy. It will be bright green in colour but should show signs of browning around the edges. Garnish with a sprig of mint and a sprinkling of grated nutmeg or pared lemon zest.

SERVE warm or at room temperature with salad and a wedge of lemon.

COOK'S TIP – This tart will serve 10–12 as a starter or vegetable dish.

Seventeenth-century Broad Bean Tart

SERVES 4–6

175g (6 oz) plain shortcrust pastry,
    made using half white and half
    wholemeal flour (see page 15)
4 tablespoons crème fraîche
juice of 1 lemon
350g (12 oz) fresh or frozen (defrosted)
    broad beans
2 eggs, beaten
large handful of chopped fresh chives
    (about 2 tablespoons)
55g (2 oz) ham, diced
salt and freshly ground black pepper

The broad bean is believed to be the original bean of Europe. Most major archaeological sites contain the remains of the broad bean which, because of its widespread distribution and capacity for being dried and transported, was a staple food, especially for the poor. Young beans were eaten raw in some countries, while older beans – those with the black spot – were only fit for boiling and then passing through a sieve to leave the tough skin behind.

Superstition surrounds the broad bean and there are numerous stories of avoidance and refusal to eat them, the commonest reason being that the souls of the dead migrate into them. But, in spite of such legends, there are many people today who are addicted to the broad bean.

The crisp texture of the uncooked bean gives this tart an unexpected crunchiness. However, you can pre-cook the broad beans if you prefer. Some cooks also prefer to skin the beans before final cooking. After all, this is not just a tart for bean addicts but for all who like a colourful tart.

Line a shallow 23cm (9 in) tart tin with the pastry and pre-bake or bake blind as directed on page 16. Pre-heat the oven to 180°C/350°F/Gas 4.

Place the crème fraîche, lemon juice and two-thirds of the broad beans in a food processor and whizz up until it forms a green mush. Spoon the mixture into a bowl, add the eggs, chives, ham and remaining beans and stir to mix. Season well with salt and pepper. Spoon the mixture into the pre-baked pastry case and bake in the oven for 30–35 minutes or until set.

SERVE warm or at room temperature.

COOK'S TIP – This tart will serve 8–10 as a starter or vegetable dish. For a starter, serve the tart with a dollop of crème fraîche, to which has been added lemon juice, chopped chives and seasoning. As a vegetable dish, serve this tart warm or cold as part of a buffet.

Carrot and Cumin Tart

SERVES 4–6

175g (6 oz) plain shortcrust pastry
   (see page 15)
25g (1 oz) butter
1 tablespoon olive oil
2 onions, finely chopped
550g (1¼ lb) carrots, cut into short thin
   strips
2 tablespoons lemon juice
1 heaped tablespoon cumin powder
2 teaspoons caster sugar
½ teaspoon salt
freshly ground black pepper
150ml (¼ pint) double cream
1 egg, plus 1 egg yolk

The Romans were clever with vegetables, experimenting in ways which now seem very sophisticated. As with many other ingredients, they saw the vegetable as the starting point for embellishment with sauces, spices, wine and other adornments in any number of ways – frying, boiling, puréeing. They shunned simple cooking and the pure taste of vegetables, and their inventiveness is reminiscent of the revival of English cooking, following the vogue for foreign travel and exotic restaurants. The carrot, like many others, fell victim to the fashion for using spices.

However, this is a simple carrot and onion purée, spiced with cumin and lemon juice. It is a versatile accompaniment to many roast and other meals; but it is also a much-appreciated vegetarian main course.

Line a shallow 23cm (9 in) round or 29½ x 20cm (11¾ x 8 in) rectangular tart tin with the pastry and pre-bake or bake blind as directed on page 16. Pre-heat the oven to 200°C/400°F/Gas 6.

Heat the butter and oil in a heavy-bottomed frying pan, add the onions and fry very gently for about 10 minutes or until soft, stirring occasionally.

Meanwhile, put the carrot strips into a colander, place over a pan of boiling water and steam for 10–15 minutes or until the carrot pieces are soft. Drain and add to the softened onion in the frying pan. Add the lemon juice, cumin, sugar, salt and pepper, give the mixture a good stir and heat gently for 2 minutes. Put the mixture into a food processor and add sufficient cream to make it work smoothly. Whizz for a few seconds until blended, then put into a large bowl. Set aside.

In another bowl, lightly whisk the egg and egg yolk together, then add the remaining cream. Add this to the carrot and onion mixture, mix well and adjust the seasoning if necessary. Spoon into the pre-baked pastry case and bake in the oven for 25 minutes or until a knife inserted into the centre of the tart comes out clean.

SERVE hot or warm, either fresh out of the oven or re-heated later.

COOK'S TIP – This tart will serve 8–10 as a starter or vegetable dish.

Onion Tart

SERVES 6–8

225g (8 oz) plain shortcrust pastry
(see page 15)

1 tablespoon chopped fresh thyme

25g (1 oz) butter

2 tablespoons olive oil

8 onions, finely sliced

salt and freshly ground black pepper

2 teaspoons caster sugar

½ teaspoon grated nutmeg

¼ teaspoon ground ginger

2 eggs, plus 2 egg yolks

425ml (¾ pint) double cream

large pinch of saffron strands

*O*nions were brought to Britain by the Romans and have been with us ever since. Valued for their medicinal, antiseptic and religious associations, they were often mentioned in rhymes and legends. Although they were eaten raw by many, their cooking qualities were quickly recognised and they became central to many cooking activities.

The secret of any successful onion tart is the slow and careful frying of the onions prior to the baking of the tart. This is an updated version of a fourteenth-century tart taken from the Forme of Cury, 1378. As this involves slicing a number of onions, it is worth putting them in the fridge overnight as the cold reduces the irritation to the eyes. Remember that the slow cooking changes the starch in the onion to sugar and, in so doing, reduces the volume by about two-thirds.

Roll the pastry out on a lightly floured surface sprinkled with the thyme and use to line a deep 23cm (9 in) tart tin. Pre-bake or bake blind as directed on page 16. Pre-heat the oven to 190°C/375°F/Gas 5.

Melt the butter and oil in a wide, heavy-bottomed frying pan (with a sealed lid) over a medium heat. Add the onion slices, sprinkle with salt and the sugar. Put the lid on the frying pan, turn the heat down low and cook for about 20 minutes – you will need to stir the onions occasionally to check that they are not sticking. Remove the lid and cook for a further 10 minutes or until the mixture has reduced down and become somewhat darker. Stir in a sprinkling of grated nutmeg (leaving the rest for the top) and the ginger and remove the pan from the heat.

Lightly beat the eggs and egg yolks together and season with a little salt and black pepper. Put the cream in a pan with the saffron, heat gently until warm, then add to the beaten eggs and stir to mix.

Spoon the onion mixture over the base of the pre-baked pastry case, then pour the egg and cream custard over the top. Bake in the oven for 25 minutes or until set and golden brown.

SERVE warm.

COOK'S TIP – This tart will serve 10–12 as a first course. If cooking in individual tartlet tins, reduce the cooking time by about 10 minutes.

Leek and Mushroom Tart

SERVES 6–8

225g (8 oz) plain shortcrust pastry
(see page15)

8 leeks

55g (2 oz) butter

6 large field mushrooms

1 tablespoon finely chopped fresh
tarragon

200g (7 oz) cream cheese

300ml (½ pint) double cream

2 eggs, lightly beaten

½ teaspoon English mustard

½ teaspoon grated nutmeg

salt and freshly ground black pepper

*L*eeks were regarded as a superior vegetable by the Romans who thought of onions and garlic as food for the poor. They savoured the more delicate flavour of the leek and used it in their dishes in large quantities. It is possible that they brought the leek to Britain and it was certainly in wide use in medieval times and a prized vegetable to serve to the wealthy. The cooks of King Richard I were adept at mixing leeks with different ingredients and mushrooms were one of their favourites, although they sometimes had problems distinguishing the edible from the non-edible. The tradition of mixing leeks and mushrooms has continued and many a modern vegetarian dish links the two. In medieval times, cooks would have used sugar (or honey), mustard and grated nutmeg. So the tradition of using herbs and spices has been kept. You can, of course, add chopped ham or bacon as is found in the well-known country dish called Likky (Leek) Pie.

Line a deep 23cm (9 in) tart tin with the pastry and pre-bake or bake blind as directed on page 16. Pre-heat the oven to 190°C/375°F/Gas 5. Place a baking sheet in the oven to get hot.

Trim the leeks by cutting off their tougher green tops and their root base. Cut into 5mm (¼ in) slices and wash thoroughly, then drain in a colander or large sieve. Melt the butter in a large heavy-bottomed frying pan. Add the leeks and fry gently until they start to go slightly soft, stirring occasionally. Break up the mushrooms into rough pieces, add to the leeks and cook for a few more minutes, stirring occasionally. Add the tarragon and cook for a further 1 minute.

Meanwhile, put the cream cheese into a large bowl and whisk until smooth, then add the cream, eggs, mustard, nutmeg and salt and pepper and mix well.

Place the leek and mushroom mixture into the pre-baked pastry case and pour the cheese mixture over the top. Place the tart on the hot baking tray and bake in the oven for 35–40 minutes until it looks set.

SERVE with a green salad or a green vegetable, such as sugar-snap peas or broccoli.

COOK'S TIP – This tart will serve 10–12 as a starter.

Salmon and Herb Tart (see page 23)

Pea and Artichoke Tart (see page 28)

Carrot and Cumin Tart (see page 30)

Apricot and Almond Tart (see page 34)

Rice Tart

SERVES 6

225g (8 oz) rich sweet shortcrust pastry
(see page 15)

85g (3 oz) butter

85g (3 oz) caster sugar

2 eggs

55g (2 oz) ground rice

300ml (½ pint) single cream

300ml (½ pint) whole milk

55g (2 oz) currants (about 2 handfuls),
(placed in a cup of boiling water, left
to cool, then strained)

½ teaspoon ground cinnamon

½ teaspoon vanilla essence

extra ground cinnamon and a few small
knobs of butter, to decorate
(optional)

Rice tarts were known in the fifteenth and sixteenth centuries, as rice was a storecupboard staple, offering the cook many opportunities for incorporating both fresh and dry ingredients. But it was an expensive import at the time and so was used sparingly, and mostly by the wealthy. This particular tart uses ground rice and is an amalgam of a number of recipes, including an old Scottish covered tart, which was stiff with thick sweet cream, spices and currants, and the more abstemious Kentish pudding pie. The latter was served during Lent when meat was not allowed and everyone was tired of weeks of fish. It has a memorable texture and taste – something like a sophisticated and creamy bread and butter pudding.

Yet another version of this tart is adapted by Mrs Beeton and is generally known as Folkestone Pudding Pie. This involves infusing the cream with a bay leaf and a large strip of lemon peel before adding to the rice mixture.

Line a deep 23cm (9 in) tart tin with the pastry and pre-bake or bake blind as directed on page 16. Pre-heat the oven to 180°C/350°F/Gas 4.

In a bowl, beat the butter and sugar together until light and shiny. Beat in each egg in turn, then put the mixture to one side.

Put the rice, cream and milk in a pan over a low heat and bring gently to the boil, stirring frequently. Turn off the heat and by this time the mixture should have thickened. Cool for a few minutes, then add the rice mixture to the butter, sugar and egg mixture and mix well. Stir in the plumped currants, cinnamon and vanilla essence. Pour into the pre-baked pastry case and, if desired, create a topping by sprinkling the top with extra cinnamon and a few small knobs of butter. Bake in the oven for about 45–50 minutes, by which time the filling should be golden brown around the edges and slightly firm to the touch. If the filling seems a little wobbly, leaving it in the oven for a few minutes, after the oven has been switched off, usually seems to do the trick.

SERVE hot or cold with thick cream.

Apricot and Almond Tart

SERVES 8

225g (8 oz) rich sweet shortcrust pastry
(see page 15)

55g (2 oz) unsalted butter

115g (4 oz) caster sugar

450g (1 lb) juicy ripe apricots, cut in
half and stoned

2 tablespoons amaretto

1 teaspoon almond essence

1 fresh sweet plain muffin about 100g
(3½ oz), crumbled (or similar amount
of Madeira cake)

55g (2 oz) ground almonds

40g (1½ oz) light soft brown sugar

*E*ver since the adulation heaped on the apricot by British kings and queens, the apricot tart has become an essential dessert for many used to good dining. The gardens of palaces and the larger houses in the south of England had apricot trees to rival any in the Mediterranean and they came to be a source of continuing envy by French chefs. Old English apricot tarts were distinctive in the way fresh apricot halves were first cooked and coated in butter and sugar. Any number of variations have been tried, usually to enhance the appearance of the tart: for example, putting fresh, stoned cherries or halved roasted almonds between each of the apricot halves.

In this tart, by including a layer of sweet almond on the pastry base, the soft caramelised apricots are more contained and delicious.

Line a shallow 23cm (9 in) tart tin with the pastry and pre-bake or bake blind as directed on page 16. Pre-heat the oven to 190°C/375°F/Gas 5.

Put the butter, caster sugar and 4 tablespoons of water in a heavy-bottomed wide pan. Heat gently until the sugar starts to turn slightly coloured, stirring occasionally. Add the apricot halves and stir to coat in the caramel mixture. Remove the pan from the heat and stir in the amaretto and almond essence.

Put the crumbled muffin, ground almonds and soft brown sugar in a bowl and mix together. Spread over the pastry base.

Lift the apricots out of the pan and place on top of the muffin and almond mixture with their rounded sides facing upwards. Scrape out all the delicious juices from the pan and pour over the apricots. Bake in the oven for 30–35 minutes or until the tops of the apricots are nicely browned.

SERVE hot, warm or cold with cream or crème fraîche.

Orange and Lemon Almond Tart

SERVES 6–8

175g (6 oz) rich sweet shortcrust pastry
(see page 15)
1 large thin-skinned navel orange
1 small thin-skinned lemon
2 eggs
175ml (6 fl oz) double cream
85g (3 oz) caster sugar
1 teaspoon almond essence
85g (3 oz) ground almonds
3 tablespoons good lemon curd
1 tablespoon light soft brown sugar

Sweet oranges did not arrive in Britain until the late sixteenth century, well in time for Nell Gwynne to show them as part of her wares. Their colour and taste rendered them great favourites with those who could afford them and there are a number of tales of seafaring captains courting the favour of kings and queens by returning with armfuls of oranges. A number of recipes for an Elizabethan orange tart have been handed down through the centuries, including this one, which has a delicious orange and lemon almond base with the easiest of lemon sauces.

Line a shallow 23cm (9 in) tart tin with the pastry case and pre-bake or bake blind as directed on page 16. Pre-heat the oven to 180°C/350°F/Gas 4.

Scrub the orange and lemon, cut them into quarters, remove and discard the peel and take out and discard any pips or end bits. Place the fruit in a food processor. Add the eggs, cream, caster sugar and almond essence and whizz up for a short burst. Whizz in the almonds in an even shorter burst and then turn the mixture into the pre-baked pastry case. Bake in the oven for 30–35 minutes or until risen and golden. Remove the tart from the oven and let it cool a bit.

Put the lemon curd and light soft brown sugar into a small saucepan and heat until liquid, stirring, then pour into a sauce jug.

SERVE either warm or cold with the lemon sauce and a dollop of crème fraîche or thick double cream.

Buttermilk Raisin Tart

SERVES 8

225g (8 oz) rich sweet shortcrust pastry
(see page 15)

85g (3 oz) caster sugar

1 heaped tablespoon plain flour

a large pinch of salt

1 teaspoon grated nutmeg, plus a pinch
for sprinkling

4 eggs, lightly beaten

1 teaspoon vanilla essence

425ml (¾ pint) buttermilk

175g (6 oz) raisins, plumped up by
placing them in hot water for a few
minutes, then draining and drying
them

Buttermilk was a staple by-product of butter-making, available in large quantities in most households in the Middle Ages. It was like a light skimmed milk, slightly sour and moved from being humdrum fare for milkmaids and shepherds to a fashionable drink for city dwellers in the seventeenth and eighteenth centuries. It then suffered a decline, particularly during the heyday of the 'milk for children' campaigns of the twentieth century. However, the drive towards less fat has given a new boost to buttermilk, which has reappeared on supermarket shelves, albeit in a less genuine format.

Like whey, buttermilk presented problems in trying to find suitable uses for it. When it was unfashionable it was often poured away. Sometimes richer buttermilk could be turned into cheese, and in other cases it found its way into tarts. The recipes for these travelled across with the Pilgrims to America, where 'buttermilk pie' came to epitomise all that was good about American family cooking.

This tart is an amalgam of a number of early recipes. It is simple to make and with no cream it is light and easily digested, and its clean-cut appearance is very inviting.

Line a deep 23cm (9 in) tart tin with the pastry and pre-bake or bake blind as directed on page 16. Pre-heat the oven to 180°C/350°F/Gas 4.

In a large bowl, stir the sugar, flour, salt and 1 teaspoon nutmeg together. Using a whisk, blend in the eggs. Add the vanilla and buttermilk and beat the whole mixture well so that there is no flour clinging to the bottom of the bowl.

Cover the bottom of the pre-baked pastry case with the plumped-up raisins and then cover the raisins with the buttermilk mixture. Sprinkle a pinch of nutmeg over the top. Bake in the oven for 30 minutes or until set.

SERVE at room temperature.

COOK'S TIP – This is one of the few tarts in this book which I can honestly say is good for you. In America, it is served with cranberries or blueberries at room temperature. Cream and crème fraîche are other good accompaniments.

Pine Nut and Cream Tart — GRANDMOTHER'S TART

SERVES 8

225g (8 oz) rich sweet shortcrust pastry
(see page 15)
115g (4 oz) roasted pine nuts
115g (4 oz) soft light brown sugar
40g (1½ oz) ground rice or plain flour
¼ teaspoon ground cinnamon
2 eggs, plus 1 egg yolk
55g (2 oz) caster sugar
1 teaspoon vanilla essence
2 tablespoons amaretto or brandy
300ml (½ pint) double cream
1 tablespoon icing sugar, to decorate

The British pine tree has been a source of pine nuts in cooking dating back to the Middle Ages and the Romans used pine nuts in both sweet and savoury dishes. British pine nuts, however, were very different from the modern imported ones, being of a rather pungent turpentine flavour and much smaller than the Mediterranean variety. The pine nuts we now use are invariably imported and are sweet, delicately flavoured and full of protein.

This is an adaptation of a tart which is steeped in history. In France, it is known as Tarte Grandmère, *and in Italy* Torta della Nonna, *and in Britain it is occasionally called Grandmother's Tart.*

This is a rather self-indulgent tart – rich and sweet, designed to please grandmothers and their grandchildren.

Line a deep 23cm (9 in) tart tin with the pastry and pre-bake or bake blind as directed on page 16. Pre-heat the oven to 200°C/400°F/Gas 6.

Spread the pine nuts over a baking sheet and place in the oven for 7–10 minutes, or until medium golden brown. Cool slightly, then chop the pine nuts roughly. Reserve 15g (½ oz) pine nuts.

Mix the remaining pine nuts with the brown sugar, ground rice or flour and cinnamon and spread over the bottom of the pre-baked pastry case.

Lightly whisk the eggs and egg yolk with the caster sugar in a bowl, then add the vanilla, amaretto or brandy and cream and mix well. Pour into the pastry case. Bake in the oven for 40–45 minutes or until the custard is firm, but with a little wobble in the middle. Watch that the pastry edges do not burn and cover the edges with foil strips if necessary.

Cool and then cover with a dusting of sifted icing sugar and place the reserved pine nuts in a small cluster in the centre of the tart.

SERVE with thick or thin cream.

Apple Snow Dumpling Tart

SERVES 6–8

225g (8 oz) rich sweet shortcrust pastry
(see page 15)

1 egg yolk, beaten

225g (8 oz) chunky orange marmalade

2 tablespoons calvados or brandy

115g (4 oz) soft brown sugar

6–8 small–medium dessert apples,
peeled and cored (but leave the
apples whole)

300ml (½ pint) fresh orange juice

900g (2 lb) windfalls or cooking apples,
peeled, cored and thinly sliced

½ teaspoon ground cinnamon

½ teaspoon grated nutmeg

finely grated rind and juice of ½ lemon

225g (8 oz) granulated sugar

300ml (½ pint) red wine or cider

3 egg whites

175g (6 oz) caster sugar

*T*aken from the sixteenth century, this recipe enables you to reserve your prime apples, such as Pippins, to create the dumplings and use windfalls to make the apple purée.

Previously the star pudding at banquets for Queen Elizabeth I, this is undoubtedly a tart for the show-off as it looks spectacular but is very easy to make. The secret is to start cooking before you need to – in fact you can cook both the purée and the dumplings the day before and then make the snow meringue topping about an hour before you want to eat it as the tart is best served warm.

Pre-heat the oven to 190°C/375°F/Gas 5.

Roll out the pastry on a lightly floured surface and use to line a deep 23cm (9 in) tart tin. Prick the base and brush with the beaten egg yolk, then pre-bake or bake blind (see page 16) in the oven for 25 minutes. Leaving the oven on, remove the pastry case and set aside.

Take the marmalade out of the jar and place it in a bowl. Stir in the calvados or brandy and half the soft brown sugar. Fill the core holes in the dessert apples with marmalade mixture (you should use up about half of the marmalade mixture). Place the filled apples in an oven-proof dish. Cover with the remaining soft brown sugar and pour over the orange juice. Cover and bake in the oven for 45–50 minutes or until the apples are just tender.

Meanwhile, cook the windfalls or cooking apples. Place them in a saucepan with the spices, lemon zest and juice, granulated sugar and wine or cider. Cover, bring to the boil, then reduce the heat and simmer for about 20 minutes or until the apples are mushy. Mash the apple mixture with a potato masher until smooth. If the purée is too runny, continue simmering further to reduce it down. Remove the pan from the heat and allow the mixture to cool and firm up.

Place the cooked whole apples in the pastry case, evenly spaced out, and fill in the gaps with the apple purée. Reserve the baked apple juices and set aside.

Whisk the egg whites in a large bowl until they are stiff and shiny. Whisk in half the caster sugar in two or three small amounts, then fold in the rest. Spoon the meringue evenly over the apples, giving a frolicsome flip upwards over each apple 'dumpling' (this helps you to locate the apples when you come to serving). Bake in the oven for 15–20 minutes or until crisp and golden.

Meanwhile, put the remaining marmalade mixture and reserved apple juices in a saucepan. Bring to the boil and bubble until the mixture is reduced and fairly thick. Pour into a jug.

SERVE the tart warm or at room temperature with the warm marmalade sauce.

Quince Custard Tart

SERVES 6–8

FOR THE QUINCE PURÉE:

4 large quinces, peeled, cored and
    cut into quarters

350g (12 oz) granulated sugar

juice of 1 lemon

one 750ml (1½ pint) bottle cheap red wine

½ teaspoon one or more of the
    following ground spices – nutmeg,
    cinnamon, mace, ginger

FOR THE PASTRY AND CUSTARD:

225g (8 oz) rich sweet shortcrust pastry
    (see page 15)

1 egg, beaten, plus 4 egg yolks

1 teaspoon cornflour

425ml (¾ pint) double cream

2 teaspoons vanilla essence

The quince was well known as early as the sixth century BC, and was prized by the Greeks, Romans and Arabs. There are many myths about the quince, many of them to do with love, marriage and fertility, and in ancient Greece the quince was substituted for an engagement ring when proposing to a betrothed; it has enjoyed an elder statesman position in the fruit kingdom ever since. Today, it is generally thought of as rare and rather special, with a unique and memorable flavour; but it is also a bit of a nuisance when it comes to cooking. Quince are hard and to get the best out of them it is necessary to cook them slowly, though there is no need to follow the instructions given to a piemaker in 1588 – that he must 'cook the quince pie well for 6 hours'.

This tart is based on the old traditions of using quinces to make a thick and delicious sweet paste – something exported from Portugal in the late Middle Ages and the forerunner of our breakfast marmalade. Many tarts and pies in Tudor and Stuart times involved the pre-cooking of the fruit in a wine syrup, reducing down to a thickish paste and then topping with a cream custard before baking.

Once the quinces have been taken care of, this is a very easy tart to make and gives a genuine taste of Old England.

Place all the purée ingredients in a large saucepan with 300ml (½ pint) water and stir to mix. Cover, bring to the boil, then reduce the heat and simmer until the quinces are soft, or at least tender, stirring occasionally.

Remove the pan from the heat and remove the quinces from the pan using a slotted spoon. Chop the quinces, then push them through a sieve.

Return the sieved quinces to the pan, bring to the boil and boil, uncovered, to reduce the mixture down, but be careful not to turn it into toffee or let it burn. Once it is the consistency of runny jam, turn off the heat and in cooling it will achieve the right consistency. The smell and taste is reward enough for the time spent waiting. Set aside.

Line a deep 23cm (9 in) tart tin with the pastry and pre-bake or bake blind as directed on page 16. Pre-heat the oven to 200°C/400°F/Gas 6.

To make the custard mix the egg and egg yolks with the cornflour in a bowl. Add the cream and vanilla essence and mix well.

Spoon the quince purée into the pre-cooked pastry case. Place the tart on a baking sheet and pour the custard mixture over the top of the quince purée. Taking care not to spill the contents, place the baking sheet and tart in the oven. Bake for 30–35 minutes or until the custard is set.

SERVE with thick cream.

COOK'S TIP – The top custard has been kept very simple, with no added spices, so that the taste of the quince can be fully appreciated with every mouthful.

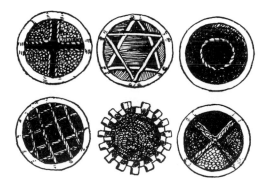

Almond Cream Custard Tart

SERVES 6

225g (8 oz) rich sweet shortcrust pastry
(see page 15)

1½ tablespoons apricot jam

2 eggs, plus 1 egg yolk

1 quantity almond milk (see recipe,
right), cooled

2 teaspoons soft butter

2 teaspoons caster sugar

*T*he almond was referred to in the Bible and, once it was introduced into Britain, the British became dependent on it for many meat and savoury dishes, often, as in the case of this recipe, using almond milk. This tart is delicious eaten warm with cream, but because it is a fairly solid tart it can be sliced up when cold.

First make your almond milk using 600ml (1 pint) liquid – I suggest three-quarters single cream to one quarter milk – 55g (2 oz) ground almonds, 1 teaspoon almond essence and 70g (2½ oz) caster sugar. Place all the ingredients in a pan and bring to the boil, then reduce the heat and simmer for 10 minutes. Remove the pan from the heat, cover and allow to cool – it will be quite thick and grainy. You can strain this, but I prefer the occasional lump of coagulated ground almond and the nice grainy texture. You can add a few drops of almond essence if you want a stronger almond flavour.

Line a deep 23cm (9 in) tart tin with the pastry and pre-bake or bake blind as directed on page 16. Pre-heat the oven to 190°C/375°F/Gas 5.

Spread the bottom of the pre-baked pastry case with the jam.

Whisk the eggs and yolk in a bowl for about 30 seconds or until they are well mixed, then add to the thick, cooled almond milk. Give it a good stir around and then put this mixture into the pastry case, spreading it out evenly. Dot the surface with knobs of butter and sprinkle with caster sugar. Bake in the oven for 25–30 minutes, or until it is set.

SERVE warm or cold with cream, amaretti biscuits or macaroons and some good sweet wine.

Sambocade – ELDERFLOWER CREAM CHEESE TART

SERVES 8

225g (8 oz) rich sweet shortcrust pastry
(see page 15)

4 eggs, separated

115g (4 oz) caster sugar

350g (12 oz) cream cheese

85g (3 oz) fresh breadcrumbs

3–4 clusters of fresh elderflowers or 1
tablespoon elderflower cordial, plus
a few clusters of flowers for
decoration (if in season)

*T*his is an unusual tart which can be baked all year round using elderflower cordial, but it is best to use fresh elderflowers when available (in June and July). It is a variation of a cheese tart using fresh or stale breadcrumbs.

Elderflowers have strong medicinal credentials and were used by witches in medieval England. Traditionally, the flowers were infused into wine, cordials and vinegars and were also used in elderflower fritters, now reappearing on modern restaurant menus. As well as being an interesting pudding tart, this tart can be eaten outside set mealtimes with a glass of elderflower wine or champagne.

Line a deep 23cm (9 in) tart tin with the pastry and pre-bake or bake blind as directed on page 16. Pre-heat the oven to 180°C/350°F/Gas 4.

In a bowl, cream together the egg yolks and sugar until almost white and shiny, then gradually add the cream cheese, beating well after each addition until well blended. Stir in the bread-crumbs and set aside.

Prepare the freshly picked elderflowers by forking the flowers off the stems. Stir the flowers or cordial into the cheese mixture.

In a separate bowl, whisk the egg whites until shiny and stiff, then fold these into the cheesy mixture. Spoon into the pre-baked pastry case. Bake in the oven for about 45 minutes or until golden brown.

SERVE warm or at room temperature with cream or crème fraîche.

Fig, Thyme, Honey and Almond Tart

SERVES 6–8

225g (8 oz) rich sweet shortcrust pastry
 (see page 15)

85g (3 oz) caster sugar

55g (2 oz) plain flour

140g (5 oz) ground almonds

2 eggs

1 teaspoon orange-flower water

½ teaspoon almond essence

110g (4 oz) unsalted butter

8–10 firm fresh figs

1 tablespoon finely chopped fresh thyme

55g (2 oz) demerara sugar

25g (1 oz) unsalted butter, cut into very
 small pieces

2 tablespoons good runny honey

juice of ½ lemon

The Romans were very keen on figs, the legend being that Romulus and Remus, the founders of Rome, were born under a fig tree. They grew more than 20 varieties, regarding it as the queen of fruits; the finest, most succulent ones went to the emperors, while the poorer quality ones went to the slaves.

Dried figs have long been used as a sweetener in the absence of sugar, but this particular tart is best made with fresh figs, which are now much more widely available, though seldom cheap. Fresh thyme is also used, as it had strong associations with the Romans who used to take baths of water and thyme to give them courage before entering battle. This tart has an almond 'frangipane' base to give body and offer a rich, contrasting flavour to that of the spiced figs.

Line a deep 23cm (9 in) tart tin with the pastry and pre-bake or bake blind as directed on page 16. Pre-heat the oven to 200°C/400°F/Gas 6.

Put the caster sugar, plain flour, ground almonds, eggs, orange-flower water, almond essence and 85g (3 oz) of the butter in a food processor and whizz until smooth and well mixed. The mixture should be quite thick. Spread the mixture in the pre-baked pastry case. Set aside.

Cut the figs into quarters and arrange them cut-sides upwards on top of the 'almond frangipane' base. Sprinkle with thyme and demerara sugar and dot with butter. Bake in the oven for 15 minutes, then put a piece of foil over the tart. Reduce the oven temperature to 180°C/350°F/Gas 4 and bake for a further 30 minutes or until golden brown.

Meanwhile, heat the honey and lemon juice together in a pan until blended. Pour into a sauce jug to serve.

SERVE warm or at room temperature with thick Greek yoghurt and the honey and lemon sauce.

Spiced Dried-fruit Tart Cooked in Ale

SERVES 6

350g (1 lb) plain shortcrust pastry, made
    with half wholemeal and half plain
    flour (see page 15)

85g (3 oz) dried apple rings

85g (3 oz) dried apricots

85g (3 oz) currants

600ml (1 pint) pale ale

3 cloves

½ teaspoon ground cinnamon

½ teaspoon grated nutmeg

finely grated zest of 1 lemon

85g (3 oz) light soft brown sugar

15g (½ oz) butter

*T*his is a tart for all seasons but, in the days before the all-year-round availability of fresh fruit we enjoy today, dried-fruit tarts came into their own in the late autumn, winter and early spring when supplies of fresh fruit dried up. Nevertheless, I think that a good dried-fruit tart can stand comparison with many fresh fruit tarts today, especially as the quality of dried fruits is now so much better than it used to be. The spices used here complete the attraction of this particular tart. To emphasise the richness of the flavours, the pastry is made with half wholemeal flour and the dried fruit is cooked in beer (pale ale). Cider can be used instead, if preferred. It is a very easy tart to make and its free-form shape makes it look warm and inviting.

Roll out the pastry on a lightly floured surface into a rough circle or square, about 38cm (15 in) diameter (you will have some pastry left over), put on a plate and put back in the fridge to chill for a further 30 minutes.

Meanwhile, make the filling by placing all the dried fruit in a saucepan with the pale ale, bring to the boil, then reduce the heat, cover and simmer for 20 minutes. Add all the remaining ingredients except the butter, stirring the sugar in last. Simmer for a further 5 minutes. Remove the pan from the heat and scoop out and discard the cloves. Drain off some of the pale ale to leave a mushy mixture. Set the filling aside to cool.

Pre-heat the oven to 190°C/375°F/Gas 5 and place a baking sheet inside to pre-heat. Prick the bottom of the pastry base all over, then top with the mushy fruit mixture. Pull up the sides of the tart and wrap around the filling. Dot the top of the tart with the butter. Carefully place the tart on the pre-heated baking sheet in the oven. Bake in the oven for 40–45 minutes or until the fruit is bubbling and the pastry is golden brown. Remember that the pastry has not been pre-cooked, so you need to ensure that it is properly cooked underneath the filling.

SERVE with crème fraîche or fresh custard.

Baked Almond Tart with Nutmeg and Sweet Wine

SERVES 6–8

225g (8 oz) rich sweet shortcrust pastry
(see page 15)

115g (4 oz) butter

115g (4 oz) ground almonds

4 eggs, lightly beaten

55g (2 oz) breadcrumbs

finely grated zest and juice of ½ lemon

½ teaspoon grated nutmeg

150ml (¼ pint) sweet wine (such as
marsala or vino santo) or sweet sherry

1 teaspoon almond essence

115g (4 oz) caster sugar

600ml (1 pint) single cream (or cream
and milk mixed)

This is a very simple almond tart, made in exactly the same way as in the Middle Ages, using melted butter as the mixing medium and stale bread as breadcrumbs. This is a particularly satisfying tart to make because you can accumulate the ingredients in an unhurried and pleasurable way and then, rather like a painter, mix them together in one single creative outpouring. Alter the measures of almond and nutmeg to suit, although too much nutmeg – thought at the time to be a powerful aphrodisiac – could leave you with post-tart fatigue!

Line a deep 23cm (9 in) tart tin with the pastry and pre-bake or bake blind as directed on page 16. Pre-heat the oven to 190°C/375°F/Gas 5.

Melt the butter in a pan, then remove the pan from the heat. Toss in the ingredients in the order given above, mixing well. You will now have a rather liquid mixture. Pour the mixture into the pre-baked pastry case. Place the tart on a warmed baking tray in the centre of the oven and bake for 45–55 minutes or until golden brown and a bit wobbly.

Glaze or decorate the tart to taste – sifted icing sugar and ground cinnamon mixed together and sprinkled over the top seem to complement the tart well.

SERVE this adaptable and rich tart warm. It is very good with a glass of Madeira.

Custard Tart

SERVES 6–8

225g (8 oz) plain shortcrust pastry
(see page 15)

600ml (1 pint) single cream

pared rind of ¼ lemon

1 vanilla pod split lengthways (or ½
teaspoon vanilla essence)

a strand of saffron

3 eggs, plus 2 egg yolks, lightly beaten

55g (2 oz) golden caster sugar

1½ whole nutmegs, freshly grated

15g (½ oz) butter for dotting on the top

The custard tart began its life in the Middle Ages in Britain and took its name from 'crustade', meaning a tart with a crust. It took many forms and is still with us in many shapes and sizes. In the Middle Ages the custard was flavoured with any number of spices and flavourings: almond, honey, cinnamon, lemon, vanilla or orange water as well as dried fruit or meat such as chopped pork. Later on in the sixteenth century, the custards were flavoured with a fruit purée – apples and pears were common – and even later a fruit purée provided the bedding for the custard on top.

The heyday of the custard tart was during the early part of the twentieth century when black and white films saw a fashion for custard-tart throwing. In some of the Keystone Studios' earliest films, it was not unusual for 1,000 custard tarts to be thrown in one scene and there developed a special kind of screen tart with a robust military-quality pastry and a runny custard with a high splat capacity.

Line a deep 23cm (9 in) tart tin with the pastry and pre-bake or bake blind as directed on page 16. Pre-heat the oven to 180°C/350°F/Gas 4 and place a baking tray inside to pre-heat.

Put the cream in a saucepan with the lemon rind, vanilla pod and saffron and leave to stand for 5 minutes. Gently heat the cream mixture until almost boiling, then remove the pan from the heat.

Meanwhile, whisk the eggs, egg yolks and sugar together in a large heatproof jug, but without producing any frothy bubbles. Pour the cream through a strainer on to the egg mixture, together with half the grated nutmeg and vanilla essence (if not using a vanilla pod). Stir up again to mix well and to make sure the eggs are not just sitting at the bottom of the jug.

Place the pre-baked pastry case on the hot baking tray and then fill the pastry case with the custard mixture – do this carefully to avoid flooding. Sprinkle more nutmeg on top and dot with the butter. Carefully replace the baking tray in the centre of the oven and bake for 30–40 minutes or until golden brown, speckled and slightly risen up in the centre.

SERVE warm or cold. This tart goes well with fruit.

COOK'S TIP – You could substitute 150ml (¼ pint) of runny honey for the caster sugar to make this tart more authentic.

Cherry Tart

SERVES 8

175g (6 oz) rich sweet shortcrust pastry
(see page 15)

450g (1 lb) cooking (sour) cherries,
stoned or a 675g (1½ lb) jar (or cans)
of dark morello cherries

150ml (¼ pint) sour cream

225g (8 oz) cream cheese

1 heaped teaspoon cinnamon

finely grated zest of 1 lemon

2 eggs, lightly beaten

55g (2 oz) light soft brown sugar

3 tablespoons good quality morello
cherry jam (preferably no-added-
sugar jam)

1 tablespoon demerara sugar mixed with
¼ teaspoon ground cinnamon, to finish

Cherries became very popular in Britain towards the end of the Middle Ages, although the Romans had culti-vated them much earlier, and they were very common in monastery gardens. They are often mentioned in folklore and have been linked to the cuckoo which reputedly stops singing only after it has eaten three good meals of cherries. The cherry is also associated with poetry, dancing, music and festivals. In some areas the end of the cherry-picking season is still celebrated on the first Sunday in August by baking small cherry pies called bumpers – eaten with a pint of ale.

One of the more successful trees taken by the early settlers to America was the cherry and today the American cherry pie epitomises all that is good in American home-making and baking. In the absence of a cherry stoner you can use a potato peeler – when pushed into the cherry you can usually take out the stone without inflicting too much damage.

Line a shallow 23cm (9 in) tart tin with the pastry and pre-bake or bake blind as directed on page 16. Pre-heat the oven to 190°C/375°F/Gas 5.

If using fresh cherries, remove the stones and stalks from three-quarters of the cherries. This requires patience but is very rewarding if undertaken sitting at a table with a good friend and sipping something reviving. If using bottled or canned cherries, drain them thoroughly and soak up any excess liquid on kitchen paper.

Place the sour cream, cream cheese, cinnamon, lemon zest, eggs and soft brown sugar in a bowl and mix well to remove all the lumps of cheese. This will produce a thickish liquid mess.

Assemble the tart by spreading a thin layer of cherry jam on the pastry base, spoon the cheese mixture over the top, then drop the prepared fresh cherries or three-quarters of the bottled or canned cherries into the liquid. They will all but disappear with just a bit of some tops showing. Sprinkle the top with the demerara sugar mixed with the cinnamon. Bake in the oven for about 35–40 minutes or until the filling has firmed up (the top of the cherries may look a little wizened, but a good dusting of icing sugar when cool will hide the wrinkles, if they worry you).

SERVE with any remaining cherries, single cream and perhaps a small glass of cherry brandy.

Pumpkin and Apple Tart

SERVES 6–8

225g (8 oz) rich sweet shortcrust pastry
(see page 15)

450g (1 lb) apples (Cox's Orange Pippins
are good), peeled, cored and thinly
sliced

225g (8 oz) pumpkin, skinned, de-seeded
and thinly sliced

2 tablespoons cornflour

½ teaspoon ground mixed spice

½ teaspoon ground cinnamon

½ teaspoon ground nutmeg

55g (2 oz) butter

115g (4 oz) light soft brown sugar

115g (4 oz) dried dates, halved

175ml (6 fl oz) double cream

2 dates, very finely chopped, mixed with
2 tablespoons demerara sugar, to
decorate

The pumpkin, like rhubarb, has both strong supporters and detractors. It has been used as a savoury vegetable, a main ingredient in soups and as an occasional ingredient in bread and tarts. Like spinach and prunes, it was one of the stalwart ingredients used for making the sticky, thick, coloured 'tart stuff' in the seventeenth century. This became glamorised when the pumpkin travelled with the Pilgrims to North America, giving rise to their much-loved pumpkin pie. One great virtue of the pumpkin is that it will absorb the flavour of whatever it is cooked with.

In the Gower Peninsula of South Wales, pumpkin and apple provide a much-loved old-fashioned tart. But if you find yourself short of a handy pumpkin, just use 1½ lb of apples instead. The addition of dates gives this tart an unexpected texture.

Line a deep 23cm (9 in) tart tin with the pastry and pre-bake or bake blind as directed on page 16. Pre-heat the oven to 190°C/375°F/Gas 5.

Place the apple and pumpkin slices in a large bowl. Mix the cornflour and spices together and sprinkle over the apple and pumpkin. Toss to mix.

Melt the butter and sugar in a wide flat-bottomed pan and add the spiced apple and pumpkin mixture. Stir over a medium heat for 1–2 minutes to ensure that all the slices are covered with the butter and sugar mixture. By this time there will be a thickish, brown, bubbling liquid. Stir in the date halves.

Pour the mixture into the pre-baked pastry case, then pour the cream over the top. Finally, sprinkle the surface with the finely chopped dates mixed with demerara sugar. Bake in the oven for 30–35 minutes or until the tart is golden brown and some of the pieces of fruit begin to look crisp.

SERVE warm or cold with cream. This tart also goes well with butterscotch ice cream.

Strawberry and Verjuice Custard Tart

SERVES 6–8

225g (8 oz) rich sweet shortcrust pastry
(see page 15)

450g (1 lb) strawberries

110g (4 oz) caster sugar

2 teaspoons lemon juice

2 teaspoons cider vinegar

55g (2 oz) plain flour

25g (1 oz) golden caster sugar

grated zest of ½ lemon

1 egg, plus 2 egg yolks

425ml (¾ pint) single cream

lemon juice and caster sugar, to serve

*T*he term 'strawberry' is variously described as reflecting the straying habit of the plant or as coming from the practice of laying straw underneath the fruit to keep it off the damp ground. The present garden and commercially grown strawberry was unknown in Britain until the nineteenth century. Prior to that, gardeners, monks and other strawberry lovers worked hard on the small wild strawberry to fatten it up a bit. Even as a small fruit it was much loved and enjoyed by itself, with wine or with cream. Even today we argue about whether it is better to leave the fruit in its pristine condition or whether to serve it with sugar, cream or wine – or even in wine.

Cooking strawberries is not a crime; they were often cooked in the past and are delicious. This tart recaptures the old traditions of steeping fruit in verjuice – sour juice for pickling and cooking made from squeezed grapes or apples. It was used until the end of the nineteenth century and was then replaced by lemon juice. To be true to the old taste, one should really use a very sharp cider, but here I have mixed lemon juice and cider vinegar in very small quantities.

Line a deep 23cm (9 in) tart tin with the pastry and pre-bake or bake blind as directed on page 16. Pre-heat the oven to 190°C/375°F/Gas 5.

Take three-quarters of the strawberries, hull them, then cut them in halves or quarters. Place them in a bowl and stir in 55g (2 oz) caster sugar. Add the lemon juice and cider vinegar, stir well, then set aside for 30 minutes.

Mix the flour, golden caster sugar and grated lemon zest in a bowl, then sprinkle over the pastry base. Drain the strawberries well, reserving the fruit and juice separately, then place the strawberries in the pastry base.

Make the egg custard by whisking the eggs, egg yolks and remaining 55g (2 oz) caster sugar in a bowl. Heat the cream in a pan until almost boiling, then gradually add the cream to the egg and sugar mixture, stirring. Add some of the juice from the strawberries (depending how much there is) and stir to mix. Pour over the strawberries in the pastry case so that some strawberries are just poking through the surface of the custard. Bake in the oven for about

35–40 minutes or until just set, well risen and golden brown in patches. Remove from the oven and allow to cool to room temperature.

While the tart cools, slice the remaining strawberries, add some lemon juice and sugar and stir to mix. Leave for a few minutes.

SERVE the tart with the sliced strawberries and some cream.

Raspberry Cream Tart

SERVES 6–8

400g (14 oz) rich sweet shortcrust
    pastry, made with added vanilla
    essence if you wish (see page 15)
675g (1½ lb) fresh, large raspberries
175g (6 oz) caster sugar, plus
    1 tablespoon caster sugar
1 egg white
425ml (¾ pint) double cream
3 egg yolks
1 tablespoon kirsch or framboise
    (optional)

*R*aspberries were first recorded as a garden fruit in Britain in 1548 and this recipe dates back to the late sixteenth and early seventeenth centuries. These early tarts would have involved a liberal use of spices and alcohol, but the use of spices became less fashionable in the eighteenth century and the natural taste of the fruit was encouraged. Raspberries seem perfect just as they are, though I have included the optional use of alcohol in the cream custard.

In many tarts and pies using fresh fruit or dried fruit, it was common to make a hole in the lid towards the end of the cooking. A cream custard made from egg and cream was then poured in through this hole and allowed to blend with the fruit and juices for a few minutes as the tart was placed once more in the oven. The result was a delightfully rich and irresistible swirly mix of fruit, juices, custard and pastry. It would almost certainly have been cooked in puff pastry but sweet shortcrust pastry is as nice, I think, and has certain practical advantages.

Roll out 225g (8 oz) pastry on a lightly floured surface and use to line a deep 23cm (9 in) tart tin. Pre-bake or bake blind as directed on page 16. Wrap and chill the remaining pastry and pre-heat the oven to 190°C/375°F/Gas 5.

Tumble the raspberries into the pre-baked pastry case and cover with 175g (6 oz) sugar. Roll out the remaining pastry for the lid, place over the raspberries and seal the edges. It will seem a bit like the Dome inside with lots of empty space. Brush the pastry lid with lightly beaten egg white and sprinkle with the remaining 1 tablespoon sugar. Place the tart in the oven and bake for 35–40 minutes.

Meanwhile, heat the cream in a pan until scalding, then pour it slowly on to the egg yolks in an oven-proof bowl, whisking all the time. Add the kirsch or framboise, if using.

Remove the tart from the oven and make a hole in the centre of the lid. Using a funnel, pour the yolks and cream mixture into the tart, being very careful not to be too impatient. Allow time for it to mingle with the raspberries. Return the tart to the oven for 10 minutes, to allow it time to heat right through, thicken and soak up the raspberry juices.

SERVE hot or cold, on its own.

Congress Tartlets

SERVES 8

225g (8 oz) rich sweet shortcrust pastry
(see page 15)

225g (8 oz) caster sugar

225g (8 oz) ground almonds

1½ tablespoons ground rice or semolina

3 egg whites

60g (2¼ oz) desiccated coconut

½ teaspoon almond essence

finely grated zest of ½ lemon

4 tablespoons good raspberry jam

Congress Tartlets are a favourite for afternoon teas served freshly baked and warm, but they can equally well be cooked as a full tart, to be served as a pudding with cream or ice cream. The taste of desiccated coconut, together with raspberry jam, will stir the memories of many. The name is thought to date from the seventeenth century when, at the end of the Thirty Years War, a Congress was held in Osnabrück, Germany. All those who attended were presented with a macaroon tart marked with a pastry cross. Some cooks still put a pastry cross on and if you have any spare pastry you may like to try it, but I prefer the filling heaped up high and beautifully browned on top. The amount given here is for eight 8cm (3¼ in) tartlet tins or one shallow 23cm (9 in) tart tin.

Pre-heat the oven to 200°C/400°F/Gas 6.

Roll out the pastry on a lightly floured surface and use to line the tartlet tins. Chill them in the fridge while making the filling. Place a baking sheet in the oven to pre-heat.

Put the sugar, ground almonds, ground rice or semolina into a large bowl. In a separate bowl, whisk the egg whites until they are frothy but still runny then add the dry ingredients from the other bowl. Stir in all but a handful of the desiccated coconut, the almond essence and lemon zest.

Take the tartlet cases out of the fridge and spread raspberry jam over their bases. Spoon the almond and coconut mixture into the tins until they are almost full, then sprinkle each with a little of the remaining coconut. Place the tarts on the hot baking sheet in the oven. Bake in the oven for 20 minutes or until the fillings are risen and golden brown. Allow to cool.

SERVE warm with cream or cold with a pot of hot tea.

COOK'S TIP – If making one large 23cm (9 in) tart, bake for a further 10 minutes or so, until the filling is risen and golden brown.

Dried Apricot Tart

SERVES 6

175g (6 oz) rich sweet shortcrust pastry
(see page 15)

FOR THE APRICOT BASE:

450g (1 lb) ready-to-eat dried apricots

115g (4 oz) caster sugar

juice of ½ lemon

2 tablespoons amaretto

FOR THE FILLING:

4 tablespoons double cream

225g (8 oz) cream cheese

85g (3 oz) ground almonds

55g (2 oz) caster sugar

2 eggs

1 teaspoon almond essence

4 tablespoons amaretto or brandy

1 tablespoon demerara sugar

A pricots first arrived in England in 1582, brought in by King Henry VIII's former gardener. They were initially not a great success. Later on in the eighteenth century, Lord Anson grew them with great success, producing his own variety – Moor Park – which was good enough to be exported world-wide.

This tart is easy to make, delicious and confirms my love affair with apricots. The new ready-to-cook apricots require no soaking and are full of rich, evocative flavours complemented so well by the easy almond and amaretto topping.

Line a shallow 23cm (9 in) tart tin with the pastry and pre-bake or bake blind as directed on page 16. Pre-heat the oven to 190°C/375°F/Gas 5.

Reserve 8 of the dried apricots and put the rest in a saucepan with 300ml (½ pint) water, the sugar, lemon juice and amaretto. Cover, bring to the boil, then reduce the heat and simmer very gently for 15–20 minutes. Remove the pan from the heat and mash very crudely with a fork or potato masher.

Put all the ingredients for the filling, except the demerara sugar, into a food processor or bowl and whizz or whisk together until well mixed.

Spoon the dark, squidgy apricot mash into the pre-baked pastry case and then spoon the cream cheese and almond filling over the top. Arrange the reserved apricots evenly around the tart and sprinkle with demerara sugar. Bake in the oven for 25–30 minutes. The filling will rise up and become golden brown in colour, leaving the apricots bubbling away in their little hollows.

SERVE hot or warm with some warm, sieved apricot jam and crème fraîche.

Maid of Honour Tartlets

SERVES 8

225g (8 oz) rich sweet shortcrust pastry
(see page 15)

½ teaspoon ground cinnamon, for rolling
out the pastry

2 egg yolks, lightly beaten

225g (8 oz) cream, cottage or curd cheese

115g (4 oz) unsalted butter, softened

2 tablespoons brandy

good pinch of salt

2 tablespoons caster sugar

½ teaspoon freshly grated nutmeg

175g (6 oz) ground almonds

finely grated zest and juice of 1 lemon

8 sliced or flaked almonds and mixed
sifted icing sugar and ground
cinnamon, to decorate

Traditionally the fare of the wealthy, especially the nobility, Maid of Honour tarts were associated with Kew and often known as Richmond Tarts. Another older term was 'daryol', although this involved a custard, as opposed to a cheese, base. It is said that these were all favourite tarts of Anne Boleyn when she was at Hampton Court Palace as a Maid of Honour to Catherine of Aragon. Through time there have been many adaptations and variations and it is up to each tart-maker to play around with the basic idea of these tarts to suit individual tastes – some, for example, are made with breadcrumbs as well as the ground almonds; others include currants. Unlike in medieval times, when cooking the fillings had to be started the day before, today we can use well-drained cream cheese or cottage cheese, making this a quite simple and easy tart to make and one that is much loved by older generations.

Roll the pastry out on a lightly floured surface sprinkled with the cinnamon and use to line the eight 8cm (3¼ in) tartlet tins. Prick the base of each tartlet and brush with a little of the egg yolks and place in the fridge, while making the filling. Pre-heat the oven to 200°C/400°F/Gas 6. Place a baking sheet in the oven so that it is hot and at the correct oven temperature when the tartlets arrive.

Put the cheese into a mixing bowl, add the butter, remaining egg yolks and brandy and beat until pale and well mixed. Stir in the salt, sugar, nutmeg, ground almonds and lemon zest and juice, mixing well.

Fill the tartlet cases with the cheese mixture and smooth over the surface, before adding a sliced or flaked almond to each tartlet as decoration. Put the filled tartlet cases on to the hot baking sheet and bake in the oven for 20–25 minutes or until risen and golden brown. Sprinkle with the mixed sifted icing sugar and cinnamon.

SERVE warm with single cream, or cold with a pot of hot tea at teatime.

COOK'S TIP – If making one large 23cm (9 in) tart increase the cooking time by about 10 minutes.

A Sixteenth-century Tart of Flowers

SERVES 8–10

175g (6 oz) rich sweet shortcrust pastry
(see page 15)

2 large handfuls of fresh flower heads
(reserving some for decoration)

55g (2 oz) caster sugar

55g (2 oz) butter

450g (1 lb) curd cheese

2 eggs, plus 1 egg yolk

finely grated zest and juice of 1 lemon

large pinch of mace

1 tablespoon light soft brown sugar
mixed with ½ teaspoon cinnamon

*T*aken from the Proper New Book of Cookerye *in the library of Corpus Christi College, Cambridge, this tart reawakens our interest in the medieval use of flowers in cooking. Often they were used for colour, decoration, their known beneficial effects on health, and less often for their flavour. With this curd tart, you have a choice of marigolds, which produce a rich golden tart, primroses, cowslips or borage. If you are short of flowers, introduce a mix of spices and dried fruit. But if you do include flowers try to reserve a few to decorate your tart.*

Line a shallow 23cm (9 in) tart tin with the pastry and pre-bake or bake blind as directed on page 16. Pre-heat the oven to 190°C/375°F/Gas 5.

Put the fresh flower heads in a saucepan of boiling water and boil for 1 minute. Take out of the water and drain thoroughly. Set aside.

Cream the caster sugar and butter together in a bowl using an electric whisk. Beat in the curd cheese until well mixed, then beat in the eggs and egg yolk. Add the lemon zest and juice, mace and cooked flowers and stir briefly. Put the mixture into the pre-baked pastry case and sprinkle with the mixed brown sugar and cinnamon. Bake in the oven for 45–50 minutes or until the tart is well risen and golden.

SERVE warm or cold with a glass of flowery sweet wine.

COOK'S TIP – To make this tart a bit special, serve on a large plate decorated with some fresh flower heads. You could also crystallise the flower heads – 'medieval style' – by dipping them in lightly beaten egg white and then in caster sugar and leaving for 30 minutes or so.

Peach and Hazelnut Tart

SERVES 8–10

350g (12 oz) rich sweet shortcrust pastry
(see page 15)

4–5 ripe peaches

3 tablespoons brandy or marsala wine

115g (4 oz) hazelnuts or ground almonds

25g (1 oz) semolina

25g (1 oz) light soft brown sugar

85g (3 oz) caster sugar

½ teaspoon ground cinnamon

beaten egg or milk, to glaze

*O*ld peach stones found in London indicate that the Romans were eating the fruit in England almost 2,000 years ago. But it was in the sixteenth century that peach-growing became well established, using imported French varieties. As with strawberries there is a reluctance to cook peaches, though they have in fact been cooked in tarts for centuries; wrapping peaches in pastry seems to encourage the release of their full flavour and the sensuous feel of their flesh.

This recipe is adapted from the seventeenth century – 'A Peach Pie: my Lady Sheldon's Receipt'.

Line a shallow 23cm (9 in) tart tin with 175g (6 oz) pastry and pre-bake or bake blind as directed on page 16. Reserve the remaining pastry and keep wrapped and chilled. Pre-heat the oven to 190°C/375°F/Gas 5.

Place the peaches in a large bowl. Pour over enough boiling water to cover and leave for 1 minute. Drain, skin, halve and stone the peaches, discarding the water, then cut them into thin slices. Place the peach slices into a bowl, spoon in the brandy or wine and give them a good stir. Set aside.

Meanwhile, roast the hazelnuts on a baking sheet in the oven for 10 minutes. Cool slightly, then grind them in a food processor until finely chopped. Reserve about 15g (½ oz) ground nuts and set aside. Put the remaining ground nuts in a bowl with the semolina and soft brown sugar, mix well, then spread over the pre-baked pastry base. Place the peach slices on top and pour over any juice and alcohol left in the bowl. Mix the caster sugar and cinnamon together, reserve about 1 tablespoon, then sprinkle the rest over the peaches.

Roll out the remaining pastry very thickly for the lid, incorporating the reserved ground nuts while rolling. Place over the tart and dampen and seal the edges. Put a slit in the centre, brush with beaten egg or milk and dust with the reserved caster sugar and cinnamon mixture. Bake in the oven for 40–45 minutes but check towards the end of this period that the tart surface has not gone too brown – if so, cover lightly with foil. The tart should be crisp on the outside with the pastry clinging to the peaches inside.

SERVE warm or at room temperature with thick double cream.

Blackberry and Apple Butterscotch Tart

SERVES 8

400g (14 oz) rich sweet shortcrust pastry
(see page 15)

3 dessert apples

225g (8 oz) blackberries, already sweet
and not 'pippy' – use frozen if fresh
are not available

finely grated zest and juice of ½ lemon

175g (6 oz) caster sugar, plus
1 tablespoon caster sugar

55g (2 oz) semolina or ground rice

55g (2 oz) soft brown sugar

1 egg white, beaten

*E*arly blackberry and apple tarts (or pies, as it is more common to call them) date back to medieval times when apple pulp was cooked alongside the blackberries. The pulp would have reduced the cooking time for the blackberries, something which is important if you want to preserve their flavour and avoid soggy, seedy blackberries and uncooked, watery and slightly sour apples.

Blackberries are thought to date from neolithic times and have become a very British and much-loved seasonal fruit, evoking memories of late summer expeditions. There was an ancient taboo about eating blackberries after 10 October, for during that night the devil was believed to stamp or spit on every blackberry bush. But by then the wild blackberries were without flavour and cooks today now turn largely to the supermarket for imported or frozen blackberries.

This tart makes use of wild, home-grown, imported or frozen blackberries. However, it is important, if picking wild or home-grown fruit, to make sure that the variety is suitable for cooking. It should be sweet, compact and free from hard pips. No amount of sugar can transform a sour, shrivelled blackberry into a luscious fruit. The semolina and brown sugar are there to soak up the delicious juices and, together with the lemon juice, to provide a rich butterscotch layer underneath.

Roll out 225g (8 oz) of the pastry on a lightly floured surface and use to line a deep 23cm (9 in) tart tin. Pre-bake or bake blind as directed on page 16. Wrap and chill the remaining pastry.

Peel, core and thinly slice the apples. Place the apple slices in a bowl with the blackberries, then add the lemon zest and juice and 175g (6 oz) caster sugar and stir gently to mix. Taste and add more sugar, if necessary. Cover with clingfilm, then give it a good stir after about 10 minutes. Leave for another 30 minutes to draw out all the juices.

Pre-heat the oven to 200°C/400°F/Gas 6 and place a baking sheet inside to pre-heat.

Mix the semolina or ground rice and brown sugar together and spoon the mixture over the base of the pre-baked pastry case. Spoon the fruit, together with its juices, over the semolina and sugar. Place a pie blackbird or an upturned china egg cup in the centre of the tart.

Roll out the remaining pastry to make a lid and place it on top of the tart, sealing well around the edges. Brush with beaten egg white and sprinkle with the remaining 1 tablespoon caster sugar to give a crisp top. Make a couple of slits in the pastry lid. Place the tart on the baking sheet in the oven and bake for 35–40 minutes or until the apples are really tender. Test for this by inserting a knife through one of the slits to see if the apple is still too crunchy. You may need to protect the edges of the pastry with foil strips towards the end of the cooking time to prevent over-browning.

SERVE warm with crème fraîche, thick cream or custard.

COOK'S TIP – This tart is ideal for a family lunch on Sunday, or any other similar occasion, when memories of childhood are likely to be revived or where those around the table have helped to pick the blackberries.

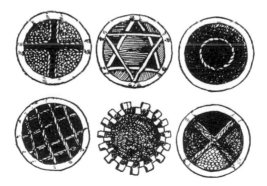

*B*y the eighteenth century, tarts and pies were becoming less fussy, sometimes less rich and more likely to resemble the ingredients first put into them. The heavily spiced mixed savoury and fruit almondy tarts of the Middle Ages were now less popular. The ready availability of cookery books encouraged gardeners and cooks alike to experiment, to widen their horizons, and to be part of the fashion for a new vegetable or fruit.

Although Britain was suffering from culinary lack of confidence – believing at the time that all things French were superior – it nevertheless continued to confirm its reputation in the pudding department: although the French outdid us in sophistication, we led the field with our majestic raised pies and tarts.

Changing dining habits in wealthier households, where lunch was the main meal, led to the growth of sweet tarts for the newly established tea with a growing range of soft fruit tarts sweetened with sugar. By the eighteenth century, sugar was no longer confined to a shelf in the locked medicine cabinet and in wealthier households it had replaced honey as the main sweetener. For the poor, sweetness was still found through honey and natural ingredients such as parsnips in the Stilton and Parsnip Tart (see page 69).

The mixture of sweet and sour, salty and bland, was a common theme when baking savoury tarts, as in the Spinach, Raisin and Potato Tart (see pages 70–1). People had had centuries of dried, pickled and salted food and they revelled in the ever-widening range of fresh ingredients, captured here in the eighteenth-century Chocolate Tart (see page 82) and many others.

In large households, pastry-making became highly specialised and separate areas would be set aside in cold north-facing rooms with marble slabs and even colder floors – ideal for nurturing the essential cold pastry hands. Better equipment became available – tin and ceramic baking dishes, copper baking sheets and, later on, the beginnings of controllable enclosed ovens.

In the nineteenth century, there was an acceleration in the production of new equipment and almost a glut of cookery books – many of them written by women for women and often aimed at the uninformed and unpretentious cook. The written recording of the recipes previously handed down from one generation to another encouraged the sense of regional culinary traditions and an awareness of earlier generations' pride in their ingredients and methods. This was manifest in the local official or unofficial competitions centred around cake- and tart-making, including that of the many-coloured northern Harlequin Tarts (see page 76).

Because of their portability and flexibility, pies and tarts held pride of place on picnics. And the growth in train travel and the long enforced station stops enabled travellers to feed one another from their picnic hampers throughout the length of their journey. Jam tarts, although a favourite in Victorian Britain, were too sticky for picnicking and so they were often given a dry meringue or pastry topping.

Refrigeration, better transport, the invention of bottled sauces and jams, canned fruits, milk and vegetables further extended the range of ingredients included in pies and tarts. But, looking back, it is clear that the most successful and enduring tarts were those based on the earliest of traditions – almonds, breadcrumbs, eggs, cream and sugar (honey or syrup), giving rise to the many versions of the Bakewell and treacle tarts, a few of which are described here.

These are the familiar comfort foods of our childhoods and favourite occasions. To try them again and to get a feel for their origins will reawaken those memories. There are also tarts here which may be less familiar but which were popular in the eighteenth and nineteenth centuries and deserve bringing back into our repertoire of old tarts today.

Fidget (Fitchet or Figet) Pie

SERVES 6–8

350g (12 oz) plain shortcrust pastry
(see page 15)

2 tablespoons olive oil

2 large onions, finely chopped

225g (8 oz) smoked streaky bacon,
chopped

450g (1 lb) crisp eating apples (about 3
medium-sized apples)

2 tablespoons finely chopped fresh parsley,
plus extra for rolling out pastry lid

1 tablespoon finely chopped fresh sage,
plus extra for rolling out pastry lid

salt and freshly ground black pepper

2 eggs, plus extra beaten egg, to glaze

150ml (¼ pint) double cream

150ml (¼ pint) dry cider

½ teaspoon grated nutmeg

*T*his is an old recipe handed down through generations of farmers' wives and it still appears in farmhouse cookery books today. There seem to be any number of versions, and many regions or towns (notably Huntingdon in Cambridgeshire) claim it as their own. There are also several explanations of the description 'fidget', one of which is the ability of the different ingredients to move around or 'fidget' inside the pie. But its really distinctive character is the combination of pork and apple, though in this instance I have used bacon instead of pork. This combination allowed farmer's wives to bake their pies knowing that the apple would keep the pie moist.

Variations of the pie allow the inclusion of different herbs and spices as well as liquids to flavour the stock. Traditionally, both mustard and vinegar have been included, but I find them too pervasive, masking the attractive mix of apple and pork or bacon. A layer of parboiled or cooked slices of potato can be included, either within the pie or as a replacement for the pastry lid.

This is a homely, old-fashioned, special-occasion pie, versatile in the opportunities it offers for serving and eating.

Roll out 225g (8 oz) pastry on a lightly floured surface and use it to line a deep 23cm (9 in) tart tin. Pre-bake or bake blind as directed on page 16. Wrap and chill the remaining pastry. Pre-heat the oven to 200°C/400°F/Gas 6.

Heat the oil in a pan, add the onions, cover and fry gently until soft, stirring occasionally. Add the bacon and continue to cook, uncovered, for 2 minutes, stirring occasionally.

Meanwhile, peel, core and thinly slice the apples. Put a layer of apple slices in the pre-baked pastry case. Top with half the bacon and onion mixture, then sprinkle with half the fresh herbs and season with salt and pepper. Add a further layer of the remaining apple slices and top with the remaining bacon and onion mixture and herbs. Season again.

In a bowl, beat the eggs, then add the cream, cider and nutmeg. Season with salt and pepper, then pour the mixture into the pastry case over the layers of apple, bacon and onion.

Take the uncooked pastry from the fridge and roll it out to make a lid, rolling the pastry out on a lightly floured surface sprinkled with finely chopped herbs, so that the herbs become embedded in the pastry. Lay the pastry lid of the tart over the filling, pinch the edges to seal, make a few slits in the pastry and brush all over with the extra beaten egg. Place the tart in the oven and bake for 15 minutes, then reduce the oven temperature to 180°C/350°F/Gas 4 and bake for a further 35–40 minutes or until golden brown.

SERVE hot with cabbage, spring greens or other green vegetables; or cold with coleslaw, plum or apple chutney and some good strong cider.

Smoked Haddock Tart

SERVES 4–6

175g (6 oz) plain shortcrust pastry
   (see page 15)
2 tablespoons chopped fresh parsley
450g (1 lb) smoked haddock fillets
150ml (¼ pint) milk
a few black peppercorns
3 bay leaves
a few sprigs of fresh parsley
55g (2 oz) butter
2 onions, finely chopped
3 tablespoons cucumber, chopped
1 tablespoon chopped fresh chives
2 tablespoons plain flour
175ml (6 fl oz) single cream
salt and freshly ground black pepper
115g (4 oz) Cheddar cheese

The smoking of fish pre-dates most other forms of preserving food, long before the Greeks and Romans, although both of these became specialist smokers and devourers of smoked fish. The Vikings and Norsemen all loved dark smoked fish, the most famous being the Arbroath smokies in Scotland, still very much in demand. Smokehouses in the Middle Ages used oak and other woods to create dark-smoked haddock and it wasn't until the middle of the nineteenth century that the milder, lighter smoked yellow haddock (the Finnan Haddock – known as haddies) became popular. It came originally from Findon village just south of Aberdeen.

It is now quite easy to find filleted smoked haddock, and it is worth making the effort to buy naturally smoked fish without the bright yellow dye. This delicious tart looks exceptionally good and is a great favourite with my own family.

Roll the pastry out on a lightly floured surface sprinkled with 1 tablespoon chopped parsley and use to line a shallow 23cm (9 in) tart tin. Pre-bake or bake blind as directed on page 16. Pre-heat the oven to 190°C/375°F/Gas 5.

Place the haddock fillets in a wide-bottomed frying pan with a lid. Cover with the milk and add the peppercorns, bay leaves and sprigs of parsley. Bring gently to the boil with the lid on, then turn the heat off and leave the pan for 5–10 minutes. Take the haddock fillets out of the pan using a slotted spoon, reserve the liquid, then break up the fish into small flakes, being sure to remove and discard any bones. Set aside.

Melt the butter in a separate frying pan, add the onions and fry for about 10 minutes or until quite soft, stirring occasionally. Add the cucumber, remaining parsley and chives, stir in the flour and cook for 2 minutes.

Strain the reserved liquid from cooking the fish. Gradually stir the strained fish liquid and cream into the onion mixture and continue stirring over a low heat until the sauce thickens. Add salt and pepper to taste, then add the cheese, reserving a handful for the top. Add the flaked fish and then transfer it all into the pre-baked pastry case. Sprinkle the tart with the reserved cheese. Bake in the oven for 30 minutes or until the tart looks risen and brown.

SERVE warm with wedges of lemon and a green vegetable.

Cherry Tart (see page 48)

Strawberry and Verjuice Custard Tart (see page 50–1)

Peach and Hazelnut Tart (see page 57)

Blackberry and Apple Butterscotch Tart (see page 58–9)

Tomato, Onion and Goat's Cheese Tart (see page 66–7)

Spinach, Raisin and Potato Tart (see page 70–1)

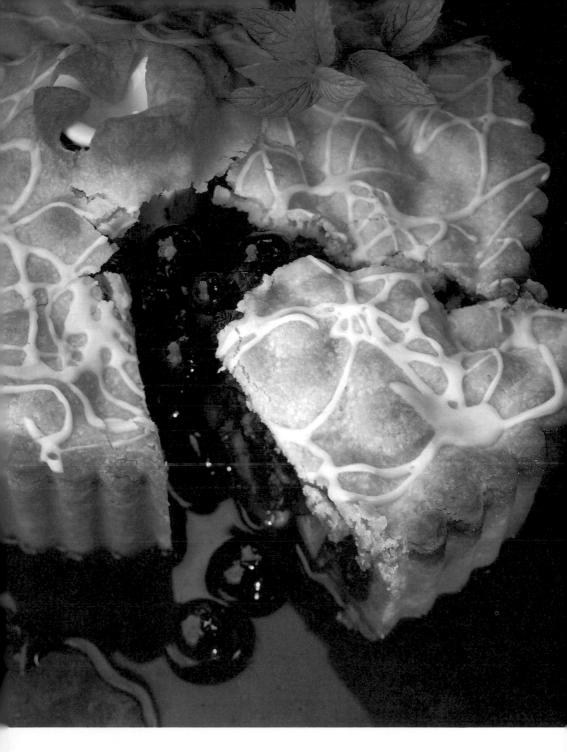

Bilberry 'Mucky Mouth' Tart (see page 86)

Rhubarb and Strawberry Tart Cooked in Beer (see page 90–1)

Eighteenth-century Three-cheese Tart

SERVES 4–6

175g (6 oz) plain shortcrust pastry
(see page 15)

115g (4 oz) Cheshire cheese

115g (4 oz) Gloucester, Leicester or
Lancashire cheese (or any similar
regional cheese of your choice)

115g (4 oz) herbed cream cheese, such
as Boursin

2 eggs, plus 2 egg yolks, lightly beaten

425ml (¾ pint) double cream

1 tablespoon sweet sherry (optional)

½ teaspoon ground mace or freshly
grated nutmeg (optional)

1 teaspoon French mustard

4 spring onions, finely chopped

1 tablespoon finely chopped fresh thyme

salt and freshly ground black pepper

Although the Romans made cheese, the revival in British cheese-making took place in the Middle Ages. Cheese-making among the rural population concentrated on hard cheeses and several kinds of soft cheese, including green cheese and spermyse (a cheese with herbs). The very first specialist cookery book on cheese was printed at the end of the fifteenth century. But during the eighteenth century, the Gentlemen Farmers began more widespread production of milk and much of this was made into butter and cheese for sending to the large towns, especially London. In particular, Cheshire became a focal point for the production and distribution of cheese; the rich grassland of Cheshire, bordering the River Dee, produced an excellent pale golden cheese, subsequently coloured artificially.

This is the easiest of tarts to make and, with its delicious herby cheesiness and oozy lumps of cheese, it can be used on any number of occasions. It would originally have included some alcohol and spices but I have left these as optional. You can choose your own regional cheeses to suit your taste or loyalties.

Line a shallow 23cm (9 in) tart tin with the pastry and pre-bake or bake blind as directed on page 16. Pre-heat the oven to 200°C/400°F/Gas 6.

Crumble the hard cheeses into small pieces and place them in a bowl. Break up and add the herbed cream cheese.

Put the eggs, egg yolks, cream, sherry, mace or nutmeg, mustard, spring onions and thyme in a separate bowl and mix well. Stir in the crumbled cheeses, season with salt and pepper, then spoon the mixture into the pre-baked pastry case. Bake in the oven for 35 minutes or until the tart looks nicely puffed up and golden brown, though the surface will quickly sink back a bit. Test with a knife that the inside is set before removing the tart from the oven.

SERVE warm or cold with a watercress or fresh tomato salad with olive oil and fresh thyme sprinkled over.

COOK'S TIP – This tart is brilliant on picnics and will serve 8–10 as a starter.

Tomato, Onion and Goat's Cheese Tart

SERVES 6–8

225g (8 oz) plain shortcrust pastry
(see page 15)

6 ripe, firm and well-flavoured tomatoes
(preferably on the vine)

2 red onions, finely chopped

2 tablespoons olive oil

2 tablespoons finely chopped fresh basil

2 tablespoons finely chopped fresh
parsley, plus extra to garnish

55g (2 oz) fresh breadcrumbs (white or
wholemeal)

3 eggs, lightly beaten

300ml (½ pint) double cream

salt and freshly ground black pepper

115g (4 oz) Cheddar cheese, grated

1 round (85g/3 oz) goat's cheese

*T*he tomato, known as the 'love apple' because of its presumed aphrodisiac qualities, originated in South America, being well known to the Aztecs. It was brought to Europe by the early Spanish explorers at the beginning of the sixteenth century but did not become popular or well used for some time. In fact, for 200 years it was grown largely for its ornamental qualities. It seems that Jewish families in Britain with their links to Mediterranean Europe were more adventurous and recipes began to appear at the beginning of the nineteenth century. But it was not until the end of that century that cartloads of the crop found their way beyond the walls of the most wealthy, and even then the tomato remained unpopular and was associated with witchcraft and disease.

Successful tomato recipes are those where the distinctive taste of the fruit surmounts the other flavours. I think this tart succeeds in this, but partly through its soft texture. You can, of course, vary the nature and quantity of the herbs to suit your own tastes.

Line a deep 23cm (9 in) tart tin with the pastry and pre-bake or bake blind as directed on page 16. Pre-heat the oven to 200°C/400°F/Gas 6.

Put the tomatoes in a bowl, cover with boiling water and leave for just over 1 minute, then lift them out with a slotted spoon. Skin and chop the tomatoes (it doesn't matter if a bit of skin gets left on one or two), then drain them in a colander or sieve to get rid of excess juices and squeeze out most of the seeds. Put them to one side.

Fry the onions gently in the olive oil in a covered frying pan for 5–10 minutes or until they are just soft, stirring occasionally. Add the herbs and breadcrumbs and stir to mix. Turn off the heat.

Put the eggs into a bowl, add the cream and salt and black pepper. Add most of the Cheddar cheese, saving 2 teaspoons for the garnish.

Spoon the onion, herb and breadcrumb mixture into the pre-baked pastry case. Add most of the tomatoes, reserving just a few for the garnish.

Pour in the cream mixture, then break the goat's cheese into small pieces and press into the cream mixture. Sprinkle with the remaining Cheddar, tomatoes and a little chopped parsley. Bake in the oven for 35–40 minutes or until the pieces of goat's cheese have browned around the edges (you may need to turn the tart round a bit once or twice during cooking).

SERVE hot or warm as a main course with courgettes or green beans and some small boiled potatoes with their skins on, or as a starter with rocket, chicory and avocado.

COOK'S TIP – This tart will serve 10–12 as a starter and may be baked in a 34 x 11cm (13½ x 4¼ in) rectangular tin.

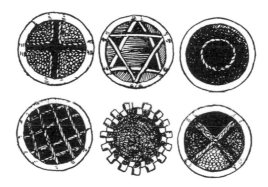

Pickled Walnut Tart

SERVES 4–6

175g (6 oz) plain shortcrust
    pastry (see page 15)
400g (14 oz) jar pickled walnuts
2 red onions, finely chopped
2 tablespoons olive oil
2 eggs, lightly beaten
300ml (½ pint) double cream
85g (3 oz) Gloucester or Leicester
    cheese, crumbled
85g (3 oz) medium Cheddar cheese,
    grated
½ teaspoon wholegrain mustard
salt and freshly ground black pepper
finely chopped chives or parsley, to
    garnish

'A woman, a steak and a walnut tree, the more you beat 'em, the better they be.' This is a Victorian tart recipe, reflecting a long history of reverence for the walnut. Pickled walnuts start life as green whole nuts, picked in high summer and pickled by first putting them in brine. They are then put in jars with vinegar, spices, peppers and garlic. Controversy surrounded the matter of pricking the walnuts with needles to ensure full absorption of the flavours, but most people who like them today are completely addicted to all pickled walnuts. They go very well in a tart.

This tart can also be baked in a shallow 34 x 11cm (13½ x 4¼ in) rectangular tart tin. If using a rectangular tin, there will be enough pastry and filling left over to make six 8cm (3¼ in) tartlets. These tartlets make excellent starters.

Line the tart tin(s) with the pastry (see above) and pre-bake or bake blind as directed on page 16. Pre-heat the oven to 200°C/400°F/Gas 6.

Empty the jar of pickled walnuts into a colander and drain off all the liquid. Chop the walnuts into small pieces (alternatively, you might prefer to give them a quick spin in the food processor). Set aside.

Fry the onions gently in the olive oil in a covered, heavy-bottomed frying pan over a low heat, until they are soft, stirring occasionally.

Place the eggs, cream, chopped walnuts, cheeses, softened onions and mustard in a large bowl and give the mixture a good stir. Season well with salt and pepper. At this stage the mixture will look rather unattractive. Spoon the mixture into the pre-baked pastry case. Bake in the oven for 25–30 minutes or until the mixture is dark and bubbling. If you have used a slim rectangular tin and have the excess pastry and filling for the tartlets, you will only have to bake them for about 15–20 minutes.

SERVE warm or cold, sprinkled with chives or parsley.

COOK'S TIP – This tart is delicious served as a starter and will serve 8–10.

Stilton and Parsnip Tart

SERVES 6–8

225g (8 oz) plain shortcrust pastry
(see page 15)

3 tablespoons finely chopped fresh
coriander, plus extra to garnish

2 tablespoons olive oil

1 large onion, finely chopped

1 large carrot, cut into small chunks

3 parsnips, peeled, cored and cut into
small chunks

1 tablespoon cumin seeds, slightly
crushed

salt and freshly ground black pepper

225g (8 oz) blue Stilton (not mature)

3 eggs, lightly beaten

300ml (½ pint) double cream

*W*hen the Great Fire of London was at its height, Boswell was seemingly unconcerned about the fate of his house, but he was very worried about his Stilton cheese, which he hurriedly buried in his garden.

The recipe for making Stilton first appeared in the eighteenth century, with the original thought to have come from the housekeeper at Quenby Hall just outside Leicester; known as Quenby cheese, it was sold to the Bell Inn in the village of Stilton, not far from Peterborough. Stilton has traditionally been eaten with something sweet – for example, port or a sweet wine. In this tart the sweetness of the parsnips fulfils this role admirably.

Parsnips have been valued since Roman times, and later, because of their capacity to mix well with honey, wine and spices, they often found themselves in puddings and pies.

Although we tend to think of parsnips as a roast vegetable, this tart will make you think again. Cumin and coriander help to accentuate the sweetness of the parsnip and the distinctive flavour of the Stilton.

Roll the pastry out on a lightly floured surface, sprinkled with 1 tablespoon chopped coriander and use to line a deep 23cm (9 in) tart tin. Pre-bake or bake blind as directed on page 16. Pre-heat the oven to 200°C/400°F/Gas 6.

Heat the oil in a frying pan, add the onion, carrot, parsnips and cumin seeds and toss them until covered in oil, then cover and cook gently until the onion is pale golden and soft, stirring occasionally. Stir in the remaining 2 tablespoons coriander and add salt to taste.

Crumble the cheese over the base of the pre-baked pastry case and cover with the cooked vegetable mixture.

Mix the eggs and cream in a jug and season to taste with salt and pepper. Pour over the vegetable mixture. Bake in the oven for 40–45 minutes or until set. Garnish with a sprinkling of chopped coriander.

SERVE warm or cold with a green leaf salad.

Spinach, Raisin and Potato Tart

SERVES 6–8

225g (8 oz) plain shortcrust pastry
   (see page 15)
25g (1 oz) butter
2 tablespoons olive oil
2 leeks or 1 onion, thinly sliced
3 cloves garlic, crushed
3 medium-sized potatoes, thinly sliced
salt and freshly ground black pepper
450g (1 lb) spinach leaves, trimmed
½ teaspoon grated nutmeg, plus extra
   for garnishing
115g (4 oz) grated Cheddar cheese
55g (2 oz) raisins, plumped up in boiling
   water for a minute or two, then drained
4 eggs, beaten
225ml (8 fl oz) single cream

Spinach became established in Britain in the mid-sixteenth century, having travelled slowly up through Europe from Spain after the Arab invasions. Regarded as the 'prince of vegetables' by the Arabs, it has long been prized for its medicinal and nutritional qualities. It is said to engender domestic harmony and lovingkindness. But spinach also has a great ability to absorb other flavours, making it a most useful tart ingredient.

This savoury tart combines the spinach with potatoes, which were not in common use in Britain until the seventeenth century. The characteristic sweetness of the raisins enhances the flavours of the vegetables. It is very good-looking and full of exciting flavours. If you are short of time, use frozen spinach, but remember to season it with a little nutmeg.

Line a deep 23cm (9 in) tart tin with the pastry and pre-bake or bake blind as directed on page 16. Pre-heat the oven to 180°C/350°F/Gas 4.

Melt the butter and oil in a frying pan, add the leeks or onion and fry gently until soft, stirring occasionally. Add the garlic and continue frying for a couple more minutes before removing the pan from the heat. Set aside.

Meanwhile, place the potatoes in a pan of boiling water, season with salt, return to the boil and simmer for 5 minutes until the potatoes are just beginning to become tender. Drain, season with black pepper and set aside.

Cook the spinach in a pan of boiling water for about 2 minutes. Drain off, squeeze out any excess water with your hands and lay out on a clean tea towel. Sprinkle with the nutmeg and leave to dry for 1–2 minutes.

Spread half the cheese over the base of the pre-baked tart case, then top with a thin layer of potatoes, followed by a thin layer of spinach. Sprinkle half of the raisins on top. Continue with one more layer in the same order, reserving a little cheese for the top, then add a final layer of the softened leeks or onions and garlic mixture.

Place the eggs in a jug and mix with the cream. Season to taste with salt and pepper and slowly pour the mixture over the tart, waiting for the mixture to seep down to the bottom layers. This requires patience and ingenuity as by this time the tin seems pretty full and solid; you can make a few holes in the mixture to enable the liquid to percolate successfully. Finish off by sprinkling over the remaining cheese and garnish with a little nutmeg. Bake in the oven for 30–40 minutes, or until set (test with a knife to check that the potatoes are soft).

SERVE hot, warm or cold.

COOK'S TIP – This makes an excellent tart when cooking a Sunday lunch or family supper, as it can be made beforehand. It will also serve 10–12 as a starter or vegetable dish.

Asparagus and Butter Cream Tart

SERVES 4–6

175g (6 oz) plain shortcrust pastry
(see page 15)

675g (1½ lb) fresh thin green asparagus
tips

55g (2 oz) unsalted butter

2 tablespoons grated onion

150ml (¼ pint) double cream

2 eggs, plus 1 egg yolk

salt and freshly ground black pepper

2 tablespoons chopped fresh dill

2 tablespoons chopped fresh chives

2 teaspoons French mustard

*M*rs Beeton described asparagus as 'belonging to the classes of luxurious rather than necessary food' and further condemned it by saying it was 'light and easily digested, but it is not very nutritious'. In the sixteenth century market gardeners became wealthy by 'forcing' the asparagus, but it did not start appearing regularly in recipes until the early eighteenth century.

Although it is possible to enjoy forced asparagus from all over the world for a longer period, this recipe is designed primarily for the small green English asparagus shoots available fresh in late spring and early summer.

Based on a traditional recipe, probably dating from the eighteenth century, it is a tart which helps you to stretch a small quantity of asparagus and enables you to make full use of the thinner spears which are otherwise difficult to handle.

Line a shallow 23cm (9 in) tart tin with the pastry and pre-bake or bake blind as directed on page 16. Pre-heat the oven to 190°C/375°F/Gas 5.

As these are thin asparagus shoots it is important that they should not be made too soggy. Steaming is the best answer. Trim the tips to lengths of no more than 12cm (4½ in), but keep the trimmings. Put the asparagus tips and the trimmings in a colander over a pan of boiling water and steam for 5–6 minutes until they are just cooked. Drain very thoroughly. Place the tips in the pre-baked pastry case like spokes in a wheel.

Melt the butter in a heavy-bottomed saucepan and fry the onion in the butter for just a few minutes until soft, stirring occasionally. Remove the pan from the heat and set aside.

In a bowl, beat together the cream, eggs and egg yolk. Season with salt and pepper, then add the cooked onion, cooked asparagus trimmings, dill, chives and mustard and mix well. Spoon the mixture over the cooked asparagus tips. Bake in the oven for 25–30 minutes or until the filling looks set.

SERVE warm or cold with a green leaf salad.

COOK'S TIP – This tart also makes a very good first course, especially accompanied by chopped walnuts mixed in oil, soy sauce and cider vinegar. It will serve 8–10 as a starter.

Irish Creamy Potato and Rocket Tart

SERVES 6–8

225g (8 oz) plain shortcrust pastry
(see page 15)

4 medium-sized old potatoes with their
skins on (approximately 675g/1½ lb)

55g (2 oz) rocket leaves, roughly
chopped

½ a whole fresh nutmeg, grated

salt and freshly ground black pepper

300ml (½ pint) double cream

*T*he potato originated in Colombia, South America, was brought to Spain in the sixteenth century and a short time later found its way to Ireland. By the end of the seventeenth century, it was established there with perhaps a third of the population living almost entirely on potatoes by the time of the Great Famine in 1840. Just before then, it was estimated that the average cottier (crofter) consumed between 7 lb and 14 lb of potatoes a day. Most potatoes were boiled or cooked on the griddle due to the lack of ovens, but wealthy households could rise to the baking of tarts.

Rocket was not popularised in the supermarkets until the late 1980s and early 1990s, but it has a long history in Britain. It was widespread in medieval monasteries and was known for its unusual flavour in cooking and for its medicinal uses.

This is a simple, very delicate and quite delicious tart which provides a trouble-free accompaniment to a large casserole or roast meal.

Line a deep 23cm (9 in) tart tin with the pastry and pre-bake or bake blind as directed on page 16. Pre-heat the oven to 200°C/400°F/Gas 6.

Wash and then cook the potatoes in a pan of boiling salted water for 15–20 minutes or until just cooked and firm enough to slice. Drain, then set aside to cool, leaving the skins on. Once cool, slice the potatoes into nice chunky slices.

Place half the rocket on the base of the pre-baked pastry case, then arrange a layer of potato slices on top of the rocket. Cover with half the grated nutmeg and season with salt and pepper. Cover with the remaining rocket and finish with the remaining potato slices. Sprinkle the potato slices with the remaining nutmeg and season again with salt and pepper. Pour the cream over the filling. Bake in the oven for 25–30 minutes or until the cream becomes golden brown in spots.

SERVE hot as part of a family lunch, supper or dinner, or cold with a rocket salad.

COOK'S TIP – You can vary the spices – for example, use a teaspoon of garam masala between the layers of potato for a robust alternative. Grated cheese can be added as a topping, but I prefer pure potato.

Plum Tart with a Rich Almond Custard

SERVES 6–8

FOR THE TART

175g (6 oz) rich sweet shortcrust pastry
(with 1 teaspoon almond essence
added with egg yolk) – see page 15

115g (4 oz) caster sugar

1 teaspoon ground cinnamon

675g (1½ lb) large ripe but firm plums,
stoned and cut into quarters
lengthwise

55g (2 oz) butter, cut into small pieces

FOR THE CUSTARD

55g (2 oz) almonds

400g (14 oz) tub of ready-made custard

1 teaspoon almond essence

When we think of plums we tend to think 'Victoria', the well-marketed plum dating from the middle of the nineteenth century, but there are many earlier high-quality plum varieties, the cultivation of which was at its peak in the seventeenth and eighteenth centuries. Although plums were grown in Roman times, it was in the Middle Ages that the plum achieved recognition, grown as it was in many monasteries. Its name was applied to any dried fruit, including sultanas, currants and raisins, so when the sixteenth-century rhyme about Little Jack Horner states that 'he stuck in his thumb and pulled out a plum' he was probably in fact pulling out a raisin.

In Victorian times, plums were more frequently cooked in pies, sometimes alongside whole almonds and chopped hazelnuts or with roasted walnuts. As fellow members of the apricot family, plums are natural bedfellows of the almonds.

Line a shallow 23cm (9 in) tart tin (or 6 tartlet tins) with the pastry and bake blind as directed on page 16. Pre-heat the oven to 190°C/375°F/Gas 5.

Mix the sugar with the cinnamon and spread two-thirds of the mixture over the pre-baked pastry case (or tartlet pastry cases).

Place the plum quarters evenly over the pastry base (about 6–8 quarters in the case of each tartlet), and then cover with the remaining sugar and cinnamon mixture. Dot each plum quarter with a small knob of butter. Bake in the oven for 30–35 minutes (less for tartlets), by which time the filling should be bubbling, dark and caramelly-looking.

Put the almonds on a baking tray and roast alongside the tart for 10 minutes. Cool slightly and grind finely in a food processor or similar.

Test the plums with a knife to see if they are soft. The plum quarters may shrivel; in that case you may wish to cover them with a sprinkling of sifted icing sugar, just before serving.

While the tart is cooking, warm the custard, almonds and almond essence in a saucepan.

SERVE the tart warm or at room temperature with the almond custard.

Chestnut and Chocolate Raisin Tart

SERVES 8

175g (6 oz) rich sweet shortcrust pastry
(see page 15)

200g (7 oz) cream cheese

two 250g (9 oz) cans sweetened
chestnut purée

2 eggs, lightly beaten

2 tablespoons brandy

115g (4 oz) raisins, plumped up for a
few minutes in hot water, then
drained and dried

115g (4 oz) dark chocolate (use a good-
quality dark cooking chocolate)

25g (1 oz) light soft brown sugar

4 tablespoons double cream

The chestnut seems to have originated in Asia Minor. It was grown by the Greeks more than 2,000 years ago and was brought to Britain by the Romans. The nut was used to make chestnut flour and early versions of the now fashionable maize polenta. In Britain, the chestnut was used primarily for feeding to animals or for roasting on grills in open fires, mostly around Christmas. Elsewhere in Europe, the chestnut was given enhanced status by being crystallised, as in marrons glacés, or made into sweet purées or put in soups, sauces and gravies. It has experienced a bit of a comeback in Britain with the revival of the combination of Brussels sprouts and chestnuts as an essential accompaniment to Christmas roast turkey.

In the world of puddings the chestnut is inseparable from chocolate and there are a number of old recipes combining the two. For this tart use good quality chestnut purée.

Line a shallow 23cm (9 in) tart tin with the pastry and pre bake or bake blind as directed on page 16. Pre-heat the oven to 170°C/325°F/Gas 3.

In a bowl, whisk the cream cheese with the chestnut purée until well mixed. Whisk in the eggs and brandy, then stir in the plumped-up raisins. Spoon the mixture into the pre-baked pastry case. Bake in the oven for 45 minutes or until well risen and light golden brown. During baking, the mixture will rise up and you will feel like panicking because there is no room for the chocolate topping, but it will sink down again. Remove the tart from the oven and set aside to cool.

Break the chocolate into pieces and place in a heat-proof bowl with the sugar and cream. Place the bowl over a pan of very hot water. Stir with a wooden spoon until smooth, then spoon the mixture onto the cooled tart. Cool to allow the topping to firm up before serving.

SERVE at room temperature, accompanied by a glass of suitable wine, such as a sauterne or monbazillac.

Harlequin Tart

SERVES 6–8

225g (8 oz) rich sweet shortcrust pastry (see page 15)

beaten egg, to glaze

2 heaped tablespoons of four of the following jams: dark cherry, blackcurrant or blackberry; apricot or marmalade; strawberry, raspberry or red cherry; gooseberry, greengage or lemon curd

The tradition of making colourful tarts dates back to the very beginnings of pastry-making when colour was used at every opportunity, even though no jam was available. In the seventeenth century, Robert May described in his book The Accomplished Cook *how to make 'the several colours of tarts'. He advocated using different fruits and then boiling them for some time, often with white wine and sugar. To enhance the different colours he suggested adding others so, for example, green codling apples would be boiled together with spinach, giving a thick, sticky and extremely tasty green 'tart stuff'. This could then be placed alongside 'black tart stuff' (prunes), orange (apricots) and red (raspberries).*

Jam as we know it began to be produced in massive quantities in the nineteenth century, when it was made using cheap fruit and vegetable pulp to serve up with bread as a main food for the poor.

This is a tart to please children and all those with memories of school tarts and home-made jam tarts, using up the pastry that might otherwise have been thrown away.

Roll out 175g (6 oz) pastry on a lightly floured surface and use to line a shallow 23cm (9 in) tart tin. Pre-bake or bake blind as directed on page 16. Wrap and chill the remaining pastry. Pre-heat the oven to 200°C/400°F/Gas 6.

When you are ready to make the tart, take out the uncooked pastry from the fridge, roll it out on a lightly floured surface and cut it into 2 lattice strips, slightly longer than the diameter of the tart tin. Cut off the ends and brush the strips with beaten egg. Place the strips over the pre-baked pastry case to cross in the centre so as to produce 4 triangular sections. Press the edges to seal. Make sure the lattice strips are thick and deep enough so that jam cannot run from one section to another. You may also like to decorate them, using the back of a knife blade.

Fill the empty triangles with the jams of your choice. Bake the tart in the oven for about 10 minutes or until the lattice strips are gently browned and the jams are bubbling nicely. Remove the tart from the oven and allow it to cool.

SERVE hot, warm or cold with fresh custard.

Bakewell Tart

*T*rying to condense an introduction to the Bakewell Tart – or, as some insist, Bakewell Pudding – into one page is not easy, for the more I've tried to seek out the genuine beginnings of the tart, the more complex the story has become. And now, with an exhibition on the subject in the House Museum in Bakewell, I am drowning in contradictory information. Until recently, the sources of information were the earliest cookery books, for example John Farley (1783) and Jane Thornton's collection of eighteenth-century Derbyshire dishes. The most popular story concerns the kitchen maid of the Rutland Arms Hotel who failed to follow the instructions given to her by Mrs Greaves, the cook, who was called away suddenly to look after some visitors. Instead of putting the egg mixture at the bottom and the strawberry jam on top, the kitchen maid reversed the process, converting a strawberry tart into a strawberry pudding. The dinner guests thought it a real improvement and so the Bakewell Tart was born. One of the guests at that dinner – a Yorkshire woman called Mrs Wilson – saw the commercial possibilities of this accidental tart, struck up a partnership with Mrs Greaves and began to sell the tarts or puddings from her own house. Within a year, Mrs Wilson, together with her husband, had bought a house in the square which soon became known as 'Ye Olde Original Pudding Shoppe'. Its fame spread and today there is fierce competition between hotels, pubs, restaurants and bakeries with tales of secret ingredients, including cucumber essence. But the original written recipe is supposed to be in a solicitor's vaults.

An historian and recent Mayor of Bakewell, Dr Trevor Brighton, has challenged the validity of the popular version of the origin of the Bakewell Tart. The original recipe is far removed from what we now regard as the authentic Bakewell Tart. The recipe given by Mrs Greaves shows this very clearly.

---

20 eggs
yolks of 12 eggs
1 lb butter, clarified
1 lb fine sugar

Mix all the ingredients and pour upon the jam in a puff pastry shell.

Bake in a quick oven in tins.

There was no almond, no flour, no milk or cream. The layer of jam was thick, sometimes as thick as 2.5cm (1 in). Subsequent recipes have included any of the following: breadcrumbs, potato, almond essence, ground almonds, flour and lemon. And it has been acknowledged that Mrs Greaves did seek variety in her puddings and experimented with additional ingredients. What has remained constant is the use of puff pastry, together with the distinctive, irregular, floppy-edged pudding shape, very unlike any other tart in this book.

Old Bakewell Pudding – Described At The Time As

'That Mysterious Bakewell Tart, or Pudding'

SERVES 6–8

175g (6 oz) ready-made puff pastry

3 heaped tablespoons good strawberry
jam

3 egg whites

115g (4 oz) butter

175g (6 oz) caster sugar

5 egg yolks

1 teaspoon almond essence

½ teaspoon icing sugar

The following two recipes cannot do justice to the prestigious and contentious legacy of this pudding, but I thought it only fair to produce one which is from Mrs Greaves's period.

Pre-heat the oven to 220°C/425°F/Gas 7.

Roll out the pastry on a lightly floured surface and use it to line a deep 23cm (9 in) tart tin. Pre-bake or bake blind as directed on page16.

Cover the base of the pre-baked pastry case liberally with strawberry jam. Set aside.

Whisk the egg whites in a bowl until they form soft peaks. Put to one side.

Melt the butter and caster sugar in a heavy-bottomed saucepan until dissolved, stirring occasionally. Remove the pan from the heat and add the egg yolks and almond essence. Mix well. Fold the whisked egg whites into the butter mixture. Mix thoroughly, then pour the mixture into the pastry case. Bake in the oven for 7–8 minutes or until the mixture has risen up and it becomes a rich golden brown (too much time and it quickly burns). Reduce the oven temperature to 180°C/350°F/Gas 4 and place a round sheet of foil over the tart to prevent it becoming too brown. Bake for a further 25–30 minutes or until set.

Remove from the oven and leave to cool. The tart will sink back on leaving the oven, but that is natural. When just warm, sprinkle with sifted icing sugar.

SERVE warm or cold with double cream, crème fraîche or custard.

A Modern Bakewell Tart

SERVES 6–8

175g (6 oz) rich sweet shortcrust pastry
(see page 15)

3 rounded tablespoons good apricot jam

115g (4 oz) unsalted butter, softened

115g (4 oz) caster sugar

3 eggs, lightly beaten

140g (5 oz) ground almonds

4 drops of almond essence

85g (3 oz) icing sugar

A more modern version leads inevitably to something like an apricot tart. It has a straight frangipane topping but an unusual addition of cooked glacé icing.

Line a shallow 23cm (9 in) tart tin with the pastry and pre-bake or bake blind as directed on page 16. Pre-heat the oven to 190°C/375°F/Gas 5.

Cover the base of the pre-baked pastry case with the apricot jam. Set aside.

Put the butter and caster sugar in a large bowl and beat together until shiny and fluffy. Add the eggs a little at a time, beating well after each addition. Using a metal spoon, fold in the ground almonds and almond essence. Spread the mixture over the jam in the pastry case. Bake in the oven for 35–40 minutes or until the filling is set. (You may well need to protect the top of the tart by covering it with foil after about 15 minutes to prevent over-browning.)

Make up the icing by mixing together the sifted icing sugar and 2 teaspoons hot water. Spread the icing over the warm tart. Return the tart to the oven for a further 5 minutes, then take it out and leave to rest for 10 minutes. The tart will now have an attractive sugar coating.

SERVE warm or cold, by itself or with crème fraîche.

Lancaster Tart

SERVES 6

175g (6 oz) rich sweet shortcrust pastry
(see page 15)

4 tablespoons lemon curd (preferably
home-made – it must be very good
quality)

1 tablespoon dark soft brown sugar

finely grated zest of 2 lemons

115g (4 oz) unsalted butter, softened

150ml (¼ pint) double cream

55g (2 oz) ground almonds

115g (4 oz) caster sugar

2 egg yolks

1 egg, lightly beaten

*T*his is another variant or cousin of the Bakewell Tart, described in slightly different forms by both Mrs Beeton and Jane Grigson. Everyone I know who likes lemon puddings loves the thought that they might dig down and discover a surprise lemony sauce or custard underneath. This pudding tart is full of delicious lemon – oozy and dark at the bottom and luminous and light at the top, yet still with a hint of the Bakewell almond about it.

Line a shallow 23cm (9 in) tart tin with the pastry and pre-bake or bake blind as directed on page 16. Pre-heat the oven to 170°C/325°F/Gas 3.

Spread the lemon curd over the bottom of the pre-baked pastry case, then sprinkle with brown sugar.

Whizz all the remaining ingredients together in a food processor until well mixed, then pour into the pastry case. Smooth the surface. Bake in the oven for 35–40 minutes or until well-risen and golden. But do check during baking that the edges of the pastry do not need protection and cover with foil, if necessary, to prevent over-browning.

You may want to decorate this tart before baking, either with a few halved almonds, or with a lattice pattern of strips made from unused pastry.

SERVE warm with some warmed lemon curd in a jug together with thick cream.

Gooseberry, Elderflower and Almond Tart

SERVES 6–8

175g (6 oz) rich sweet shortcrust pastry
(see page 15)

450g (1 lb) gooseberries

2 tablespoons elderflower cordial

115g (4 oz) granulated sugar

115g (4 oz) ground almonds

115g (4 oz) caster sugar

finely grated zest of ½ lemon

2 eggs, plus 1 egg yolk

150ml (¼ pint) double cream

Perhaps because of their associations with favourite kitchen gardens or their short season, coming at the height of summer, gooseberries are seen as quintessentially English and have been appearing in tart recipes from the early seventeenth century. This particular recipe brings together the favourite historical accompaniment to gooseberries – elderflower – and the staple almonds and cream. This gives a delicious blend of the not-so-sweet, the sweet and the creamy. Out of season you can use canned gooseberries or you could replace fresh gooseberries with fresh plums or blueberries.

Line a shallow 23cm (9 in) tart tin with the pastry and pre-bake or bake blind as directed on page 16. Pre-heat the oven to 190°C/375°F/Gas 5.

Wash and top and tail the gooseberries. Place them in a saucepan with the elderflower cordial, granulated sugar and 150ml (¼ pint) water and bring gently to the boil, stirring occasionally. Cover and simmer for 3–4 minutes or until the gooseberries are softly poached but still intact. Using a slotted spoon, lift out the gooseberries into a bowl, and put to one side. Turn up the heat and let the cooking liquid boil and reduce in quantity until it becomes thicker and more syrupy. Spread the gooseberries over the bottom of the pre-baked pastry case and spoon over the syrupy mixture.

In a bowl, mix together the almonds, caster sugar and lemon zest.

In a separate bowl, whisk the eggs and egg yolk together, then add the cream and whisk to mix. Fold in the ground almond mixture and spoon this over the gooseberries. Bake in the oven for 30 minutes, or until the tart is firm and golden brown.

SERVE with crème fraîche and, if you have some, a glass of home-made elderflower champagne.

Chocolate Tart

SERVES 10

175g (6 oz) rich sweet shortcrust pastry
(see page 15)

250g (9 oz) very best dark chocolate
(continental brand, preferably)

350ml (12 fl oz) double cream

½ teaspoon ground cinnamon or ½
teaspoon good instant coffee

2 eggs, plus 1 egg yolk

*C*hocolate was first sold in England by a Frenchman in *1657 and it quickly became fashionable, leading to the growth of chocolate houses – meeting places for the influential. This chocolate was a thick drink made with milk and eggs and its consumption was, for a long time, confined to the wealthy – women especially. Chocolate was credited with many health-giving properties, including its ability to improve fertility and the chances of producing twins.*

The eighteenth century saw a dramatic increase in the use of chocolate in sorbets, soups, puddings and tarts. The recipe I have used here dates from that century. It is a very simple ganache of boiled double cream and melted chocolate, which is then added to beaten eggs. This is a rich, sumptuous tart, and its dark appearance lends itself to decoration and adornment of your choice.

Line a shallow 23cm (9 in) tart tin with the pastry and pre-bake or bake blind as directed on page 16. Pre-heat oven to 180°C/350°F/Gas 4.

Chop the chocolate into small pieces, either by hand using a thick kitchen knife, or put it into the food processor and chop using the pulse button. Put it into a large bowl.

In a saucepan, heat the cream just to boiling point, then take it off the heat immediately and pour the cream into the bowl over the chopped chocolate. Whisk the cream and chocolate together, using a fork or hand whisk. You will notice the mixture becoming darker and you will think it is about to set. But it won't. Whisk in the cinnamon or instant coffee, then put the mixture to one side and leave until tepid.

In a separate bowl, beat the eggs and egg yolk together for just a few seconds. Continue beating while you pour in the tepid melted chocolate and cream ganache. Scrape the sides of the bowl so that all the delicious chocolate is mixed with the eggs. The mixture will now be quite liquid. Pour the chocolate mixture into the pre-baked pastry case. Bake in the oven for 20–25 minutes or until set, but with the centre still looking a bit soft and wobbly.

SERVE at room temperature with a bowl of fresh mixed berries such as blackberries, blueberries and raspberries.

Lemon Pudding Tart

SERVES 6

175g (6 oz) rich sweet shortcrust pastry
  (see page 15)
300ml (½ pint) thick double cream or
  crème fraîche
55g (2 oz) butter, softened
55g (2 oz) golden caster sugar
3 eggs, plus 2 egg yolks
finely grated zest and juice of 2
  unwaxed lemons
6 amaretti biscuits, crushed
1 tablespoon demerara sugar (optional)

*L*emons first began to be imported in small quantities in the thirteenth century, sometimes fresh, but more often they were made into a succade – a kind of marmalade. Lemons and oranges became more popular and widespread in Britain during the seventeenth and eighteenth centuries and it was soon found that, when combined with butter, cream and sugar, both fruits produced particularly delicious tarts.

This tart is an early version of today's restaurant staple – caramelised lemon tart. Covering the hot cream filling with demerara sugar gives it a particularly good colour.

Line a shallow 23cm (9 in) tart tin with the pastry and pre-bake or bake blind as directed on page 16. Pre-heat the oven to 180°C/350°F/Gas 4.

Heat the cream in a pan until hot but not boiling. Remove the pan from the heat.

Meanwhile, beat the butter and sugar together in a bowl until shiny, then add the eggs, egg yolks, lemon zest and juice and crushed biscuits and mix well.

Beat the lemon mixture into the hot cream until well mixed. Pour the mixture carefully into the pre-baked pastry case and sprinkle with demerara sugar if using. Bake in the oven for 25–30 minutes, or until the filling is firm when you gently shake the tart.

SERVE hot or warm with a good ice cream.

Canterbury Pudding Tart

SERVES 6–8

225g (8 oz) rich sweet shortcrust pastry
(see page 15)

5–6 good dessert apples (depending on
size), peeled, cored and quartered

finely grated zest and juice of 2 lemons

4 eggs

175g (6 oz) caster sugar

55g (2 oz) butter, melted

100ml (3½ fl oz) double cream

25g (1 oz) demerara sugar

½ teaspoon ground cinnamon

*Y*et another apple tart? But wait until you taste it. This is a rich, creamy, lemony tart with a chunky apple centre and crunchy caramelised slices around the edge. Any good dessert apple can be used for this as long as it is not too mealy or mushy. Coarsely grating the apple as well as finely grating the lemon zest complements the nature of the centre of the tart. In a way, this tart is akin to the official French Apple Tart, which has a base of pre-cooked apple purée, but the grated apple, cream, lemon and egg mixture in this tart is so much more tasty.

It would be nice to think that weary pilgrims to Canterbury were handed a slice of this tart at the end of their travels, but according to local sources the Canterbury Pudding, in its many guises, became distinctive only in the mid-nineteenth century.

Line a deep 23cm (9 in) tart tin with the pastry and pre-bake or bake blind as directed on page 16. Pre-heat the oven to 200°C/400°F/Gas 6. Place a baking sheet in the oven to pre-heat.

Coarsely grate two-thirds of the apple quarters into a bowl. Add the lemon zest and juice and stir to mix. Thinly slice the remaining apple quarters and put to one side.

In a bowl, beat the eggs and caster sugar together for 2 minutes. Add the melted butter, cream and grated apple mixture and mix well. Pour the mixture into the pre-baked pastry case and arrange the remaining slices around the edge in a slightly overlapping ring. Sprinkle them with demerara sugar and cinnamon. Place in the centre of the oven on the baking sheet and bake for 40–45 minutes, or until the sliced apples look soft and caramelly and the centre of the tart is tinged golden.

SERVE warm with thick cream or a good vanilla ice cream.

Raspberry and Rice Pudding Tart

SERVES 6–8

175g (6 oz) rich sweet shortcrust pastry
  (see page 15)

115g (4 oz) short-grain (pudding) rice

425ml (¾ pint) milk

300ml (½ pint) single cream

55g (2 oz) butter

85g (3 oz) caster sugar, plus 2 teaspoons
  caster sugar

3 eggs

finely grated zest of ½ lemon

450g (1 lb) raspberries – reserve a few
  for decoration

sprinkling of lemon juice

3–4 tablespoons double cream

freshly grated nutmeg, to finish

I first tasted this tart in a pub in Swaledale, but its origins in Britain are further north in Scotland, the natural home of the wild as well as the cultivated raspberry. We continue to find wild raspberries in woods and on heaths but, like the ancient Greeks who first cultivated them, we now cultivate them for varieties of size and taste.

In the past, raspberries would usually be cooked by themselves in raspberry tarts, but the addition of a thick and creamy rice pudding topping complements the raspberries well. For some, this brings back early memories of rice pudding with a dollop of raspberry jam in the middle. This old, simple, but deliciously rich recipe is adapted from Eliza Acton (1845).

Line a shallow 23cm (9 in) tart tin with the pastry and pre-bake or bake blind as directed on page 16. Pre-heat the oven to 170°C/325°F/Gas 3.

Put the rice into a saucepan with the milk and cream. Bring slowly to the boil, then reduce the heat and simmer gently for 12–15 minutes, by which time the rice should be just about tender. Remove the pan from the heat, add the butter and 85g (3 oz) sugar and stir until the butter and sugar have dissolved.

Beat the eggs in a bowl and add these to the rice with the lemon zest, mixing well.

Roughly crush the raspberries in a bowl. Place them in the pre-baked pastry case and sprinkle with the remaining two teaspoons of sugar and the lemon juice.

Spoon the rice pudding over the raspberries, and then spoon the double cream on top. Sprinkle the top with freshly grated nutmeg. Bake in the oven for 30–35 minutes, when a nice speckled golden skin should have appeared. Rice pudding skin-aholics will know exactly when the tart is done to perfection!

SERVE hot or warm with cream and a raspberry sauce, and decorate with the reserved whole raspberries.

Bilberry 'Mucky Mouth' Tart

SERVES 6–8

350g (12 oz) rich sweet shortcrust pastry
(see page 15)

2 large dessert apples, peeled, cored and
thinly sliced

225g (8 oz) caster sugar

juice of ½ lemon

1 heaped tablespoon finely chopped
fresh mint

675g (1½ lb) bilberries (blueberries)

115g (4 oz) icing sugar, sifted

a few fresh mint leaves, to decorate

*F*or many centuries, mint – an important ingredient in
this tart – was believed to be an aphrodisiac, but it is
included here because it highlights the delicate flavour of
the bilberry. In Ireland, the gathering of bilberries is associated with courting, starting on the Sunday closest to the
first day of August. Others regard mint as a stimulant to the
brain and as an aid to digestion – further reason for giving
this attractive tart a go.

This recipe was given to me by Rosie Lafin, Catering
Manager of the National Trust's Penrhyn Castle Tea Rooms
in North Wales, where it is one of the most popular items on
their menu; the recipe comes from the National Trust's own
collection of Victorian recipes. It takes its name from the
children's habit of collecting bilberries and shoving handfuls
of them into their mouths – with predictable results.

Roll out 225g (8 oz) pastry on a lightly floured surface and use to line a deep 23cm (9 in) tart
tin. Pre-bake or bake blind as directed on page 16. Wrap and chill the remaining pastry. Pre-
heat the oven to 190°C/375°F/Gas 5.

Place the apple slices in a bowl and sprinkle with half the sugar and the lemon juice. Toss to
mix and leave for 20 minutes. Using a slotted spoon, place the apple slices in the pre-baked
pastry case. Mix the mint with the bilberries and then put them on top of the apple slices.
Sprinkle with the remaining sugar and juices from the apples. Place a pie blackbird, upturned
china egg cup or similar in the centre of the tart.

Roll out the remaining pastry for the lid and place over the filling, sealing the edges. Make a
slit in the centre of the pastry lid. Bake in the oven for 35–40 minutes or until the apple slices
are soft (check with a knife through one of the slits). Remove from the oven and allow the tart
to rest and cool.

Place the icing sugar in a bowl and slowly add a few teaspoons of very hot water, mixing until
you have the right consistency to drizzle over the pastry crust in no particular pattern.
Decorate with fresh mint leaves.

SERVE warm or at room temperature with cream or vanilla ice cream.

Yorkshire Curd Tart

SERVES 6–8

225g (8 oz) rich sweet shortcrust pastry
(see page 15)

115g (4 oz) butter

85g (3 oz) caster sugar

225g (8 oz) curd cheese

115g (4 oz) seedless raisins soaked in 4
tablespoons brandy (overnight if you
can remember)

40g (1½ oz) fresh white breadcrumbs

pinch of salt

freshly grated nutmeg, to taste

2 eggs, well beaten

soft brown sugar and a little ground
cinnamon, to finish

Well known throughout Yorkshire in tea rooms, bakeries and butchers, Yorkshire Curd Tart has become an institution. In shops, it is sometimes sold in the form of tartlets, sometimes with a pastry lid and often sitting next to a line of sausages and pork chops in a butcher's shop. A number of cookery writers have given their own versions of curd tart. It remains popular because of its interesting texture and flavour and also because it is so easy to cook. I've pepped it up a bit by first soaking the raisins in brandy, though this is not necessary. I think it's best cooked slightly less than you think it needs so that it has a squidgy consistency and clings to the tongue.

Line a deep 23cm (9 in) tart tin with the pastry and pre-bake or bake blind as directed on page 16. Pre-heat the oven to 190°C/375°F/Gas 5.

Cream the butter and caster sugar together in a bowl until pale and shiny. Add the curd cheese, raisins, breadcrumbs, salt, nutmeg and eggs and mix well. Spoon into the pre-baked pastry case and sprinkle the top with brown sugar and cinnamon. Bake in the oven for 25–30 minutes or until well risen and nicely browned. Keep an eye on the pastry edges – they may need to be protected by covering them with a narrow strip of foil to prevent over-browning.

SERVE warm or cold with single cream.

COOK'S TIP – Yorkshire Curd Tarts are very good for picnics as they are firm and tasty.

Treacle Tart

SERVES 10

225g (8 oz) rich sweet shortcrust pastry
(see page 15)
280g (10 oz) golden syrup (about 6
tablespoons)
175ml (6 fl oz) double cream
2 eggs, lightly beaten (save a little for
brushing on the lattice strips)
finely grated zest and juice of 1 lemon
55g (2 oz) ground almonds
125g (4½ oz) fresh breadcrumbs
1 large cooking apple, peeled, cored and
finely chopped

Treacle, as we know it in Britain today, is the sugar syrup first produced as a by-product from sugar refining and production in the nineteenth century. It soon replaced honey as a cooking ingredient, being sweeter, more convenient, easier to get hold of and cheaper to buy.

Nevertheless, the treacle tart is based on the very earliest tart-making traditions of using honey and stale bread-crumbs. The recipe of this treacle tart is described by Theodora Fitzgibbon as originating in a hotel in Bray-on-Thames in Berkshire. Other variations make great use of lemon zest and lemon juice.

The recipe given here combines the best and simplest of school tarts with just a touch of luxury and sophistication to make it irresistible.

Roll out the pastry on a lightly floured surface and use to line a deep 23cm (9 in) tart tin. Pre-bake or bake blind as directed on page 16. While the pastry is cooking, roll out any pastry leftovers into narrow strips for the lattice top and keep on a plate in the fridge. Pre-heat the oven to 200°C/400°F/Gas 6.

Place the syrup in a pan and heat gently until warm.

In a bowl, mix the cream and most of the beaten eggs together, then add the lemon zest and juice and warm syrup and mix well.

In a separate bowl, mix together the almonds, breadcrumbs and apple. Make a well in the centre and pour in the syrup mixture. Stir until the mixture is well mixed, then pour into the pre-baked pastry case.

Lay the chilled pastry strips across the top of the tart in criss-cross fashion, chopping off and sealing the edges by pinching them together with fingers and thumb. Brush the pastry lattice with the remaining beaten egg. Bake in the oven for 25–30 minutes or until golden brown.

SERVE warm or cold and with vanilla sauce, custard or ice cream.

Norfolk Treacle Tart

SERVES 6–8

175g (6 oz) rich sweet shortcrust pastry
   (see page 15)
115g (4 oz) unsalted butter
8 tablespoons golden syrup
2 eggs, beaten
4 tablespoons double cream (or single
   cream if you prefer)
finely grated zest of 2 lemons

*O*f the many versions of treacle tarts, this Norfolk version is particularly well known and was a favourite of Charles Dickens. It is a bit unusual in that it contains no breadcrumbs.

Line a shallow 23cm (9 in) tart tin with the pastry and pre-bake or bake blind as directed on page 16. Pre-heat the oven to 200°C/400°F/Gas 6. Put a baking sheet in the oven to pre-heat.

Gently warm the butter and syrup together in a pan – just enough for the butter to melt but not letting the mixture get too hot. Remove the pan from the heat and allow the mixture to cool a little.

In a bowl, whisk the eggs, cream and lemon zest together. Gradually whisk in the warm butter and syrup mixture, then pour the mixture into the pre-baked pastry case. Place the tart on the baking sheet in the oven and bake for 25–30 minutes or until the centre is set.

SERVE warm or cold with crème fraîche or ice cream.

Rhubarb and Strawberry Tart Cooked in Beer

SERVES 8–10

450g (1 lb) rich sweet shortcrust pastry (see page 15)

550g (1¼ lb) trimmed rhubarb (about 5–6 sticks), cut into small chunks

115g (4 oz) light soft brown sugar

300ml (½ pint) beer (pale ale or bitter)

225g (8 oz) strawberries, hulled and halved

55g (2 oz) fresh breadcrumbs (white or brown)

finely grated zest of ½ lemon

25g (1 oz) demerara sugar

beaten egg, to glaze

small sprinkling of caster sugar and ground cinnamon, to finish

1 dessertspoon cornflour

*R*hubarb is a very British food, provoking love and loathing in equal measure. Very few of us escaped rhubarb in our childhood when it was second to apples as an ingredient in tarts and pies. It was first introduced into Britain in the seventeenth century, but only became fashionable as a tart ingredient at the end of the eighteenth century, reaching its greatest popularity in the nineteenth century. After some time in the doldrums, it is now experiencing something of a revival. Traditionally it has been cooked with elderflowers or strawberries and in beer, as in this tart. The strawberries bring colour and texture and accentuate the lemony tartness of the rhubarb. The lovely rhubarb juices are used to make a sauce. The cooked tart will look very rustic and inviting and, once cut, will ooze a few juices, but somehow it doesn't matter when the flavour, texture and appearance are so wonderful.

Roll out the pastry on a lightly floured surface to a large round about 38cm (15 in) in diameter. Place the pastry round in the fridge to chill for 30 minutes. Note that in this recipe the pastry is *not* pre-baked.

Pre-heat the oven to 190°C/375°F/Gas 5 and place a lightly oiled large baking sheet in the oven to pre-heat.

Place the rhubarb, soft brown sugar and beer in a saucepan. Bring gently to the boil, cover and simmer for about 7 minutes or until the rhubarb is soft but still has some texture. Remove the pan from the heat and strain the rhubarb very thoroughly, saving the juice and rhubarb separately. Put the rhubarb in a bowl with the strawberries and stir to mix.

Put the breadcrumbs, lemon zest and demerara sugar in a separate bowl and mix well.

Place the rhubarb and strawberry mixture in the centre of the pastry, then cover with the breadcrumb mixture. Pull the sides of the pastry up and around (but not completely over) the filling, pinching it into a rough shape – remember it is meant to be rustic-looking. Brush all over with the beaten egg and sprinkle with the caster sugar and cinnamon. Place the tart on the pre-heated baking sheet in the middle of the oven and bake for about 30 minutes or until the pastry is golden brown. Remove the tart from the oven and leave to cool on the baking sheet.

Put the cornflour in a saucepan, add 1 tablespoon reserved rhubarb juice and stir until well blended. Gradually stir in the remaining rhubarb juice, then heat gently, stirring constantly, until the sauce thickens sufficiently.

SERVE the tart warm with the hot sauce and thick cream.

COOK'S TIP – I find this tart looks particularly inviting when placed on a round wooden breadboard, surrounded with a few fresh strawberries.

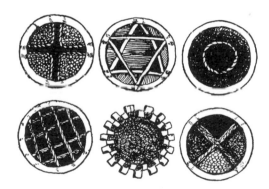

Bread and Butter Pudding Tart

SERVES 4–6

175g (6 oz) rich sweet shortcrust pastry (see page 15)

85g (3 oz) currants

85g (3 oz) sultanas

115g (4 oz) fresh breadcrumbs

1 teaspoon grated nutmeg

425ml (¾ pint) double cream

1 strip of pared lemon rind

85g (3 oz) caster sugar

85g (3 oz) butter, softened

3 eggs, lightly beaten

½ teaspoon vanilla essence

2 tablespoons brandy (rum, marsala or sweet sherry, if no brandy)

1 tablespoon demerara sugar

a few pieces of bread crust (optional)

a few small knobs of butter

This is an adaptation of the 'bread cheesecake' described by Elizabeth Raffold in her book The Experienced English Housekeeper, *published in 1799. It is a recipe which combines many culinary wares from the past and will delight all those who remember bread and butter pudding with affection. In the past, it was a way of using up the stale penny loaves, the staple food of most poor households of the time. Fortunately, and especially if they lived in the country, they were rarely short of cream for the rich custard.*

You can vary the amounts and types of fruit and add more alcohol if you wish. It is such an easy and unusual tart and is more flexible than straight bread and butter pudding. Whatever its nutritional value, it is a comforting tart and good for the psychological health of all who eat it. The secret is not to cook it too long, so that you have a wonderfully gooey centre with a crunchy golden top.

Line a deep 23cm (9 in) tart tin with the pastry and pre-bake or bake blind as directed on page 16. Pre-heat the oven to 190°C/375°F/Gas 5.

Plump up the currants and sultanas by immersing them in boiling water in a bowl for 2–3 minutes, then drain and mix with the breadcrumbs and half the nutmeg. Set aside.

Heat the cream in a pan with the strip of lemon rind until the cream is just below boiling point. Remove the pan from the heat, then remove and discard the lemon rind, add the breadcrumb mixture and mix well. Set aside.

Put the caster sugar and butter into a large bowl and beat with an electric whisk for 2 minutes or so, until pale and shiny. Add the eggs, vanilla essence and brandy and whisk until it is all absorbed. Add the breadcrumb mixture and give it all a good stir, by which time it should be looking firm. Spoon it into the pre-baked pastry case and sprinkle the top with the demerara sugar and nutmeg. If you wish to add interest to the texture, press a few small strips of bread crust into the top so that they are just showing. Dot with butter and bake in the oven for 25–30 minutes or until the surface is golden brown and the crusts are just beginning to turn dark brown.

SERVE warm or cold with custard or cream and a glass of brandy or marsala.

Raisin, Orange and Cinnamon Tart

SERVES 8

280g (10 oz) rich sweet shortcrust pastry (see page 15)

3 tablespoons cornflour

1 teaspoon ground cinnamon, plus extra for decoration

finely grated zest and juice of 1 orange

finely grated zest of 1 lemon

juice of 2 lemons

115g (4 oz) light soft brown sugar

pinch of salt

350g (12 oz) seedless raisins (soaked in boiling water for 1 minute, then drained and dried)

55g (2 oz) walnuts, finely chopped

a little milk, to glaze

This is a simple tart which is easy to make and offers a welcome break from some of the more indulgent tarts described elsewhere in this book. In earlier times, it would have been made with butter and real flour, as opposed to cornflour, but I use the latter as it guarantees no lumps and allows the full flavour of the fruit to come through.

Roll out 175g (6 oz) pastry and use to line a shallow 23cm (9 in) tart tin. Pre-bake or bake blind as directed on page 16. Wrap and chill the remaining pastry. Pre-heat the oven to 190°C/375°F/Gas 5.

Blend the cornflour, cinnamon, fruit zests and juices in a saucepan. Add 300ml (½ pint) water, the sugar, salt and raisins and stir to mix. Cook very slowly over a gentle heat until the mixture thickens, stirring constantly, then continue to cook for a further 2 minutes to ensure that the cornflour has been cooked through, stirring. Add the walnuts, stir to mix, then remove the pan from the heat and leave to cool.

Spoon the raisin mixture into the pre-baked pastry case. Roll out the remaining pastry to make a lid, dampen the edges at the rim of the tart tin, place the pastry lid on top and press to seal the edges. Prick the pastry lid with a fork and brush all over with a little milk. Sprinkle with a little cinnamon. Bake in the oven for 30–35 minutes or until golden.

SERVE hot or warm with cream.

COOK'S TIP – This tart makes a good picnic tart, being so easily transported (in which case serve it with a good, nutty, sweet wine).

Manchester Tart

SERVES 8–10

225g (8 oz) rich sweet shortcrust pastry
(see page 15)

FOR THE FILLING:

115g (4 oz) stale white breadcrumbs

425ml (¾ pint) single or double cream

150ml (¼ pint) whole milk

3 bay leaves

grated zest of 1 lemon

55g (2 oz) caster sugar

4 tablespoons brandy

1 tablespoon cocoa powder for the
chocolate version (optional)

3 egg yolks

4 tablespoons apricot, strawberry or
greengage jam

FOR THE MERINGUE TOPPING:

3 egg whites

175g (6 oz) caster sugar

Also known as Manchester Pudding or Queen of Puddings Tart, this recipe embraces the earliest of tart traditions in its use of breadcrumbs, but it has a distinctly Victorian feel to it. The story associated with it is that when Queen Victoria made a royal visit to Manchester, the humble, everyday local pudding was glamorised for her visit with the addition of a meringue topping.

For many of us, the Manchester Tart was served up as a regular school pudding, with many different names and fillings, including lemon curd, and toppings like chocolate blancmange decorated with 'hundreds and thousands'. A more upmarket chocolate and apricot version was served up at Cheltenham Ladies College. The recipe given here, however, is adapted from the original Queen Victoria version. It is a tart to be devoured immediately.

Line a deep 23cm (9 in) tart tin with the pastry and pre-bake or bake blind as directed on page 16. Pre-heat the oven to 180°C/350°F/Gas 4.

Place the breadcrumbs in a saucepan, add the cream, milk, bay leaves, lemon zest and caster sugar and stir to mix. Bring to the boil, then reduce the heat and simmer gently for 5 minutes, stirring occasionally. Remove the pan from the heat, then remove and discard the bay leaves and stir in the brandy (and cocoa, if making the chocolate version). At this stage the mixture will be something like porridge. Add the egg yolks and beat well in.

Spread the jam over the base of the pre-baked case. Spoon the soggy breadcrumb mixture over the jam. Bake in the oven for 45 minutes, by which time the mixture will have risen and be golden in colour, but will still have a slight wobble in the middle. Remove from the oven.

Whisk the egg whites in a bowl until soft peaks form. Whisk in half the sugar and beat again until very shiny. Fold in the remaining sugar using a metal spoon and spread the meringue over the top of the breadcrumb filling.

Return the tart to the oven for 15–20 minutes or until the topping is crisp and golden.

SERVE hot or warm with single cream.

COOK'S TIP – If you run out of time, or find meringues too fiddly to make, you can eat the tart plain (leaving the tart in the oven for 10 minutes extra). Sprinkle some grated nutmeg or ground cinnamon on top of the baked plain tart just before serving.

Burnt Cream Tart

SERVES 6–8

175g (6 oz) rich sweet shortcrust pastry
   (see page 15)
1 vanilla pod, split lengthways (if no
   pods are available, double the
   amount of vanilla essence)
70g (2½ oz) caster sugar
5 egg yolks
300ml (½ pint) double cream
150ml (¼ pint) full cream milk
1 teaspoon vanilla essence
2 tablespoons light soft brown sugar or
   golden caster sugar (for the 'burnt'
   caramel topping)

This recipe dates back to the early eighteenth century and was first thought to come from Scotland. It found its way into recipe books in the nineteenth century and by the twentieth century was known more consistently as Crème Brûlée Tart.

When cooked in Scottish households, the cream would be burnt by covering it with sugar and then holding a shovel full of red-hot coals above it. One young male devotee of his family's Aberdeenshire version of burnt cream took the recipe with him when he went up to Trinity College, Cambridge in the 1860s. The College rejected his recipe at first but when he returned to the College as a Fellow a few years later, they accepted it, turning it into their own and embellishing each tart or pot of burnt cream with the College's own crest. However, other Cambridge colleges insist that they were the true inventors of burnt cream.

Some people are wary of cooking burnt cream, but it is one of the easiest tarts to make, demanding only a minute or two of careful handling at the end. This tart can be prepared a day in advance, with the 'burning' taking place just before eating.

Line a shallow 23cm (9 in) tart tin with the pastry and pre-bake or bake blind as directed on page 16. Pre-heat the oven to 180°C/350°F/Gas 4.

Place the caster sugar in a bowl. Rub the split vanilla pod and shake the seeds into the sugar. Add the egg yolks and mix together well. Set aside.

Put the cream and milk in a heavy-bottomed saucepan and heat gently until almost boiling. Slowly strain this mixture through a wire sieve, a few dribbles at a time, on to the egg yolk mixture, whisking gently. Whisk in the vanilla essence, then pour the mixture into the pre-baked pastry case. Bake in the oven for 40–45 minutes or until the filling is set and a knife inserted in the centre comes out clean (protect the pastry edges by covering them with crumpled foil, if necessary, to avoid over-browning).

Remove the tart from the oven and allow it to cool completely, then refrigerate for at least 1 hour (it is possible to refrigerate the tart longer if prepared a day in advance).

Manchester Tart (see page 94–5)

Burnt Cream Tart (see page 96–7)

Courgette, Garlic and Blue Cheese Tart (see page 101)

Sultana Meringue Tart (see page 104–5)

About 30 minutes before the tart is to be eaten, pre-heat the grill to high. Sprinkle the soft brown or golden caster sugar over the cold custard, coming right up to the edges. Protect the pastry edges by covering them with foil, then place the tart under the hot grill until the sugar melts and is bubbly. This should take no more than 1 minute – any longer and you are in danger of burning too much and curdling the custard. Place the tart in a cool place for 10–15 minutes to encourage the caramel topping to become crisp.

SERVE with a few fresh raspberries, blackberries or bilberries and some cream.

COOK'S TIP – In the winter, raisins soaked in brandy offer an unusual lure to the burrowing teaspoon. Other recipes include fresh or crystallised ginger, which does add zest but I find it detracts from the rich creaminess of the filling.

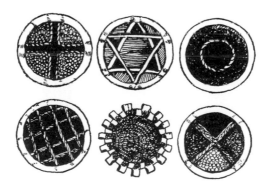

*L*ooking back to earlier centuries inspires a reflective and charitable reassessment of British cooks – their ingenuity and determination to produce something special out of unpromising ingredients, with the most limited equipment and in often uncongenial and unpleasant conditions. The twentieth century, however, seems to have seen something of a decline, with a shedding of traditions and a greater reliance on instant foods, including the ready-made pie and tart.

Through the pleadings of cookery writers there is at last a growing recognition that we neglect the past at our peril and that the centuries of rural and country traditions must not be allowed to disappear. All pie and tart makers remain grateful to the work of such organisations as the Women's Institute, publications like the *Farmers Weekly*, and all other sources of traditional recipes. Their value came to the fore during the periods of the two World Wars, when their natural frugality and flexibility reinvigorated a languishing inventiveness with ever diminishing sources of supply, illustrated here with the famous Lord Woolton Pie (see page 102). Comfort was found, too, in the reawakening interest in regional recipes, some of which are described here.

However, it would be unrealistic to expect past attitudes and approaches to be maintained when the need is no longer there. Modern tarts can embrace both the past and the present through change and adaptation. The twentieth century saw many fashions and an acceleration in the range of ingredients and these are reflected in the mix of tarts and pies in this section. But what is worth hanging on to from these earlier, leaner periods is the stimulus to creativity that comes from having to 'make do' and to try things unsupported by any recipe – a wonderful leap in the dark. The tarts using dried ingredients offer such an outlet for creativity, transforming something withered and unappetising into something grand and magnificent.

The reactions to earlier privation were bold and exciting, jolting lazy cooks into the dinner party habit where everything was for show and to impress. The arrival of green peppers on the supermarket shelves unleashed a love of the salad, perhaps to accompany Hungarian goulash or *coq au vin* and then to be followed by lemon meringue pie, pear and chocolate tart or an apricot and almond tart. These and other tarts of the 1960s and 1970s have become establishment figures, adding greatly to the range of familiar comfort foods.

More recently, there has been a plea for us all to stand up for the very best of ingredients and to re-establish the seasonal nature of our cooking, revelling in the freshly picked blackberries or raspberries, the first asparagus and the last of the apples. There are tarts here which are purely and simply the final flowering of a perfect seasonal fruit or vegetable – the Plum and Almond Tart (see page 119) and the several versions of the apple tart, for example. All these conjure up days of lingering in orchards, gardens and beside hedgerows, picking some things which are truly British, not thinking that these would one day find their way into an Old British Tart.

Sausage and Mustard Tart

(see page 15)

SERVES 4–6

175g (6 oz) plain shortcrust pastry
(see page 15)

two 425g (15 oz) cans butter beans or
haricot beans, rinsed and drained

3 tablespoons French mustard

2 tablespoons tomato ketchup

3 tablespoons single cream

salt and freshly ground black pepper

8 skinless pork chipolata sausages

2 tablespoons demerara sugar

1 tablespoon lemon juice

1 teaspoon Worcestershire sauce

Sausages have been with us since the times of the ancient Greeks, with the Romans developing the range and types of sausage until they came up against a problem: the conversion of Rome to Christianity meant that the ancient pagan phallic rites associated with the sausage were now unacceptable. Moreover, many sausages contained blood, the consumption of which was forbidden by the Bible. It is interesting that from then on the growth in the use and eating of sausages became a worldwide phenomenon.

The distinguishing feature of British sausages is the inclusion of bread and cereals, a practice which began in the nineteenth century. Sausages were cased in parts of the body – usually the intestines – of the sheep, pig, calf or ox, although nowadays much of the casing or skin is made from collagen or cellulose.

This tart is nostalgic comfort food for all of us still addicted to sausages but who seldom own up. It's good for a brunch to impress guests young and old, or for lunches, suppers and picnics.

Line a shallow 23cm (9 in) tart tin with the pastry and pre-bake or bake blind as directed on page 16. Pre-heat the oven to 190°C/375°F/Gas 5.

Put the beans, 2 tablespoons of mustard, the tomato ketchup, cream and salt and pepper in a food processor and blend together to form a purée. Spread the mixture evenly over the bottom of the pre-baked pastry case.

Arrange the sausages over the mixture so that they are evenly spaced, fanning them out from the centre like spokes of a wheel and pressing them into the mixture so that only a little of each sausage is visible. Cover with greased foil and bake in the oven for 35 minutes. Remove the tart from the oven, remove the foil and then turn the oven temperature up to 200°C/400°F/Gas 6.

Mix together the remaining mustard, sugar, lemon juice and Worcestershire sauce and, using a pastry brush, brush the mixture over the tart. Return the tart to the oven and bake for a further 10 minutes or until nicely browned.

SERVE hot with some gently fried onions or brown gravy. It is also excellent as a picnic tart.

Welsh Leek, Bacon and Goat's Cheese Tart

SERVES 6–8

225g (8 oz) plain shortcrust pastry
(see page 15)

1 tablespoon olive oil

15g (½ oz) butter

3 leeks, washed, trimmed and thinly
sliced

225g (8 oz) rindless streaky bacon, finely
chopped

1 tablespoon finely chopped fresh parsley

salt and freshly ground black pepper

2 eggs, plus 1 egg yolk

425ml (¾ pint) single cream

175g (6 oz) fresh goat's cheese (Welsh,
if possible)

55g (2 oz) walnuts, finely chopped

½ teaspoon grated nutmeg

The Welsh leek lost its place to the daffodil as the national emblem of Wales when Edward was installed as Prince of Wales in 1911, but on St David's Day it is still often worn in buttonholes in preference to the daffodil. The leek has had to fight to win approval as a main cooking ingredient in most of Britain, often being thought of simply as an addition to or substitute for onions in dishes such as stews. But it has a long and distinguished history, being widely used and well regarded by the Romans in their own cooking traditions. Now that it is so accessible almost all year round, it is again being used more and more.

Line a deep 23cm (9 in) tart tin with the pastry and pre-bake or bake blind as directed on page 16. Pre-heat the oven to 200°C/400°F/Gas 6.

Heat the olive oil and butter in a heavy-bottomed frying pan, add the leeks and fry very gently for 5 minutes, stirring occasionally. Add the bacon and continue frying until the leek is soft and the bacon is not quite crisp, stirring occasionally. Add the parsley and season with salt and black pepper. Remove the pan from the heat and set aside.

In a bowl, mix together the eggs, egg yolk and cream and season, if necessary. Break up the goat's cheese into small pieces.

Put the walnuts in the base of the pre-baked pastry case. Spoon in the leek, bacon and parsley mixture, add the goat's cheese and finally pour in the cream mixture. Sprinkle the surface with the nutmeg. Bake in the oven for 30–35 minutes or until the tart looks set and the cheese is nicely browned.

SERVE hot, warm or cold. This tart goes well with boiled new carrots or sweet sugar-snap peas.

Courgette, Garlic and Blue Cheese Tart

SERVES 6–8

225g (8 oz) plain shortcrust pastry
  (see page 15)
1 teaspoon mustard powder
675g (1½ lb) small courgettes
2 tablespoons olive oil
25g (1 oz) butter
finely grated zest and juice of ½ lemon
salt and freshly ground black pepper
6 cloves garlic, finely chopped
2 eggs, plus 2 egg yolks
300ml (½ pint) soured cream
300ml (½ pint) double cream
175g (6 oz) blue cheese (or other cheese
  if preferred)
courgette flowers or fresh chives,
  to garnish

This is a tart to commemorate all that Elizabeth David did in the 1950s and 1960s to awaken our senses by pleading for vegetables as worthy of separate and special treatment. The courgette reflects this hoped-for transition admirably.

Prior to the writings of Elizabeth David, the courgette was known as a marrow, usually grown to enormous sizes, clogging up the harvest festival displays in churches, before being stuffed with mince.

Here, the combination with garlic and lemon prevents the courgette slipping back into the gloomy days of the tasteless marrow and reminds us of Mediterranean sunshine. The use of blue cheese is a reminder that Britain has a long tradition of making blue cheese. You may prefer ordinary Cheddar or goat's cheese, but I think blue cheese really sets this tart apart as something rather special.

Roll out the pastry on a lightly floured surface sprinkled with the mustard powder and use to line a deep 23cm (9 in) tart tin. Pre-bake or bake blind as directed on page 16. Pre-heat the oven to 200°C/400°F/Gas 6 and place a baking sheet inside to warm.

Blanch the courgettes by dropping them into a pan of boiling water for 1½ minutes. Drain on kitchen paper and cut into thin slices.

Heat the oil and butter in a large pan, add the courgettes, lemon zest and salt and pepper, and fry until the courgettes are softened, stirring occasionally. Add the garlic, then turn up the heat a little and stir vigorously so that all the courgette slices are covered with bits of garlic. Remove the pan from the heat and stir in the lemon juice and more salt to taste. Set aside.

In a bowl, mix the eggs and egg yolks together, then add the two types of cream. Crumble in the blue cheese, add the courgette mixture and stir to mix it all together. Adjust the seasoning if necessary, then pour the mixture into the pre-baked pastry case. Bake in the oven on the baking sheet for 25–30 minutes (possibly a bit longer) or until firmly set and golden brown. A skewer or knife inserted in the centre should come out clean.

SERVE hot or warm with a salad of sliced tomato, drizzled with olive oil and freshly ground black pepper and covered with chopped chives. Garnish with courgette flowers, if you have them, or fresh chives.

Lord Woolton Pie

SERVES 6–8

225g (8 oz) plain shortcrust pastry
(see page 15)

2 tablespoons finely chopped fresh sage

675g (1½ lb) mixed root vegetables such
as turnip, carrot, potato and swede,
peeled and finely chopped

salt and freshly ground black pepper

6 spring onions, chopped

2 onions, finely chopped

3 tablespoons finely chopped fresh
parsley

115g (4 oz) butter

2 heaped tablespoons plain flour

425ml (¾ pint) milk

175g (6 oz) Cheddar cheese, grated,
plus a little extra to sprinkle on top

½ teaspoon English mustard

fresh parsley sprigs, to garnish

*W*hen British men were called up to fight in the First World War (1914–18) it was found that about half of them were suffering from malnutrition and in some cases were unfit to serve. From the 1930s onwards, successive governments took on the role of 'Food Nanny', giving advice and suggestions about how to improve our diet. Certainly compared with our European neighbours we consumed very little fruit, fish or vegetables. This nannying reached its peak during the Second World War (1939–45) when food of all kinds was scarce and when nothing could be wasted. It was a time when everyone was urged to dig up their garden lawns and flower beds and plant vegetables instead, and when the thought of simply enjoying food was a thing of the past. Dried eggs, dried milk and fatless pastry became the main base ingredients of any tart.

Lord Woolton, then Minister of Food, was keen for the nation to use its resources wisely and in 1940 the Ministry of Food produced this recipe.

Roll out the pastry on a lightly floured surface sprinkled with 1 tablespoon chopped sage and use it to line a deep 23cm (9 in) tart tin. Pre-bake or bake blind as directed on page 16. Pre-heat the oven to 190°C/375°F/Gas 5.

Cook the vegetables in a pan of lightly salted, boiling water for a few minutes only, or until just soft. Drain, return the vegetables to the pan, add the spring onions, onions, parsley, remaining sage and salt and pepper and mix well. Spoon the vegetable mixture into the pre-baked pastry case and set aside.

Melt the butter in a pan, stir in the flour and cook for 1 minute, stirring to ensure the flour has cooked properly. Gradually stir in the milk, then bring slowly to the boil, stirring until the sauce thickens. Stir in the cheese, mustard and salt and pepper to taste. Pour the cheese sauce over the vegetables in the pastry case and sprinkle a little grated cheese on top. Bake in the oven for 35–40 minutes or until the surface is set and nicely browned.

SERVE hot with a green vegetable and garnish with a sprig or two of parsley.

COOK'S TIP – This tart also makes an excellent dish to accompany a roast meal – perfect for Sunday lunch. It will serve 10–12 as an accompaniment.

Cumbrian Tart

SERVES 8

175g (6 oz) rich sweet shortcrust pastry
  (see page 15)
350g (12 oz) good raspberry jam
2 tablespoons golden syrup
25g (1 oz) caster sugar
55g (2 oz) butter
140g (5 oz) desiccated coconut
1 egg, lightly beaten

This is a truly delicious 'northwest' version of Bakewell Tart which is so easy to make. It is very sweet and, being so popular with children, is fairly regarded as nursery food, though I think it has quite a sophisticated demeanour. Made from desiccated coconut which came to the fore in Britain during the last war (along with dried milk and dried bananas), this is just the kind of tart some of us remember from childhood and schooldays.

Line a shallow 23cm (9 in) tart tin with the pastry and pre-bake or bake blind as directed on page 16. Pre-heat the oven to 190°C/375°F/Gas 5.

Spread the jam on the base of the pre-baked pastry case and set aside. In a saucepan, gently melt the syrup, sugar and butter together, stirring occasionally. Take the pan off the heat and stir in the coconut and egg. Spread the mixture on top of the jam. Bake in the oven for 30 minutes or so, or until the top of the mixture is invitingly crisp and golden brown.

SERVE hot or warm with normal nursery food accompaniments such as custard, evaporated milk or vanilla ice cream.

Sultana Meringue Tart

SERVES 6–8

175g (6 oz) rich sweet shortcrust pastry
  (see page 15)

FOR THE FILLING:
85g (3 oz) sultanas
3 tablespoons brandy (or rum)
1 heaped tablespoon caster sugar
1 heaped tablespoon cornflour
½ teaspoon ground cinnamon
½ teaspoon freshly grated nutmeg
large pinch of salt
400ml (14 fl oz) double cream
4 egg yolks

FOR THE MERINGUE TOPPING:
3 egg whites
175g (6 oz) caster sugar

I describe this as a 1960s English old tart. It's not really very old, but it is nevertheless steeped in memories of an era when we saw an end to the old restricted attitudes and ingredients of the war years. This was a time when cookery writers such as Elizabeth David, Jane Grigson and Robert Carrier were opening doors into experiences full of colour and excitement. Tentative would-be cooks ventured upon their first dinner parties. Exciting dishes from far-off places started to appear – bortsch, stuffed aubergines, chilli con carne, together with new puddings so much more adventurous than those we had known at home or school. Alcohol, too, was now more readily available to liven up a recipe and make cooks feel they were breaking new ground.

Although very much a 1960s tart, this has a strong ring of much earlier times with its use of dried fruit, alcohol and spices, but is given the 1960s finishing touch with the bold meringue topping.

Line a shallow 23cm (9 in) tart tin with the pastry and pre-bake or bake blind as directed on page 16. Pre-heat the oven to 180°C/350°F/Gas 4.

Put the sultanas in a bowl with the brandy, stir to mix and leave to soak for 30 minutes.

Place the sugar, cornflour, spices and salt in a bowl over a saucepan of simmering water. Add a small quantity of the double cream and mix to a smooth paste, being careful to get rid of any lumps in the cornflour. Add the remaining cream, stir well, then continue gentle occasional stirring with a wooden spoon until the mixture is smooth but thick. Remove the bowl from the heat.

Whisk the egg yolks in a separate bowl, then dribble the egg yolks into the cream mixture, whisking all the time. Return the bowl to the pan of simmering water and cook for a few more minutes, stirring, until the mixture becomes thick, but be careful not to let the mixture boil. Remove the bowl from the heat, stir in the sultanas and brandy, then set aside to cool, but stir occasionally to prevent a skin forming.

Whisk the egg whites in a large bowl until they reach the soft peak stage. Add half the sugar in 2–3 batches, whisking well, then fold in the remaining sugar using a metal spoon.

Put the sultana cream mixture into the pre-baked pastry case. Cover with the meringue, making sure it goes right up to the edges of the tart. Fluff it up with a fork. Bake in the oven for 15 minutes or until the meringue is golden brown and crisp to the touch. Remove from the oven and let it cool.

SERVE lukewarm or cold, with cream or crème fraîche.

COOK'S TIP – This recipe may be baked in eight 8cm (3¼ in) tartlet tins.

Banana, Butter and Meringue Tart

SERVES 6–8

225g (8 oz) rich sweet shortcrust pastry
(see page 15)

FOR THE FILLING:
6 firm bananas
55g (2 oz) butter
55g (2 oz) light soft brown sugar
juice of 1 lemon
1 egg, plus 3 egg yolks
55g (2 oz) caster sugar
225ml (8 fl oz) double cream
½ teaspoon vanilla essence

FOR THE MERINGUE TOPPING:
3 egg whites
115g (4 oz) caster sugar

*T*he banana came originally from India with the earliest trees dating back several thousand years but it was generally not thought possible to grow it in mainland Europe. In Britain, we were dependent on unripe bananas being brought by sailing ships, with the first bunches arriving in Smithfield market in the seventeenth century. Their rarity in Britain ensured that they did not enter cooking recipes for some time. Indeed, it was not until the advent of refrigeration at the end of the nineteenth century that we could rely on a regular and affordable supply of bananas.

Thus most banana tart recipes are from the twentieth century, their fame as a tart ingredient spreading as a result of their happy marriage with ice cream in such delicacies as knickerbocker glories. Now, the banana is associated with the American banoffee pie – a kind of banana cheesecake.

Line a deep 23cm (9 in) tart tin with the pastry and pre-bake or bake blind as directed on page 16. Pre-heat the oven to 200°C/400°F/Gas 6.

Peel and cut the bananas in half and then slice in half lengthwise. Melt the butter in a frying pan and fry the banana slices for 2 minutes on each side or until golden. Cover with the soft brown sugar and lemon juice and put the lid on the pan. Cook very gently for 1 minute to melt the sugar, then remove the pan from the heat and set aside.

Whisk the egg, egg yolks and caster sugar together in a bowl. Set aside.

Put the cream and vanilla essence in a pan and heat gently until almost boiling. Add the cream to the egg and sugar mixture and stir together.

Place the buttery bananas with their sweet brown juices in the base of the pre-baked pastry case, then pour the cream and egg mixture over the bananas. Bake in the oven for 30 minutes.

Towards the end of this cooking time, make the meringue topping. Whisk the egg whites in a bowl until they reach the soft peak stage and whisk in half the caster sugar in 2 or 3 batches. Fold in the remaining sugar using a metal spoon.

When the baking time is complete, remove the tart from the oven and turn the oven temperature down to 180°C/350°F/Gas 4. Allow the tart to cool for a few minutes and then top with the meringue mixture, making sure the meringue goes right up to the edges. Return the tart to the oven and bake for a further 15 minutes, or until the meringue seems golden and crisp. The end result is 'over-the-top perfection'.

SERVE warm or cold by itself, or with single cream.

COOK'S TIP – You could, if you wish, leave out the meringue stage and enjoy a straight banana and custard tart, but it lacks the oomph that the meringue gives.

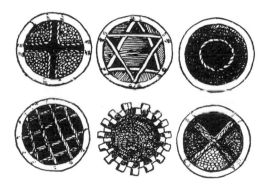

$\mathcal{A}$ 1960s $\mathcal{P}$ear and Chocolate $\mathcal{T}$art

SERVES 6

175g (6 oz) rich sweet shortcrust pastry
(see page 15)

FOR THE PEAR FILLING:

3 dessert pears, peeled and cored, but
left whole

300ml (½ pint) red wine (or water)

3 tablespoons medium sherry

juice of ½ orange

2 heaped tablespoons dark soft brown
sugar

½ teaspoon ground cinnamon

½ teaspoon ground cloves

2 tablespoons redcurrant jelly

125g (4½ oz) plain or milk chocolate
digestive biscuits

55g (2 oz) dark chocolate, chopped into
chunks

FOR THE CHOCOLATE CUSTARD:

225ml (8 fl oz) double cream

115g (4 oz) good-quality dark cooking
chocolate, broken into squares

1 teaspoon vanilla essence

1 egg, plus 1 egg yolk, lightly beaten

1 heaped tablespoon caster sugar

sifted icing sugar, to decorate

The pear was much preferred to the apple by the Greeks and Romans and has enjoyed waves of popularity throughout Europe – in Britain, this reached a high point in the nineteenth century when it was referred to as pearmania. The problem with pears – and there are now many varieties – is that it is not easy to be sure when they are ripe and their period of perfect ripeness may last for just a few hours; for this reason most cautious fruiterers and supermarkets keep very hard, teeth-crunching varieties which do not always bake well.

Line a shallow 23cm (9 in) tart tin with the pastry and pre-bake or bake blind as directed on page 16. Pre-heat the oven to 200°C/400°F/Gas 6.

Place the pears in an oven-proof baking dish. Add the wine, sherry, orange juice, sugar, spices and redcurrant jelly and give it a good stir. Cover and bake in the oven for 25–30 minutes or until the pears are cooked and tender. Remove the pears from the dish using a slotted spoon, then slice each pear lengthwise and put on one side. Boil the poaching liquid in a pan until it reduces and thickens, then turn off the heat.

Roughly chop the digestive biscuits and spread the biscuits and chocolate over the base of the pre-baked pastry case. Spoon over 3 tablespoons thickened poaching liquid, then place the pears on top 'face-down' with the narrow ends meeting in the middle of the tart. Set aside.

Put the cream, chocolate and vanilla essence in a saucepan and heat gently until the chocolate is dissolved, stirring occasionally. Remove the pan from the heat and cool slightly, then add the beaten egg and egg yolk and stir to mix. Spoon the mixture on top of the pears, filling in the gaps but leaving the rounded pear 'bottoms' still exposed. Sprinkle with caster sugar to encourage the pears to 'glaze'. Bake in the oven for 25–30 minutes or until the custard is mottled all over and feels set. Remove from the oven and set aside to cool, then sprinkle with sifted icing sugar.

SERVE warm or cold with any remaining poaching liquid or with cream.

Oatmeal, Apple and Syrup Tart

SERVES 8–10

175g (6 oz) rich sweet shortcrust pastry (see page 15)

55g (2 oz) oatmeal

1 egg white, beaten

450g (1 lb) eating apples (about 3 medium-sized apples)

300ml (½ pint) sweet cider or water

½ teaspoon ground cloves

1 teaspoon ground cinnamon

25g (1 oz) butter, cut into small pieces

55g (2 oz) light soft brown sugar

25g (1 oz) fresh white breadcrumbs

55g (2 oz) sultanas

3 tablespoons golden syrup, warmed

This is a wartime (1939–45) recipe based on one from a book of country recipes in the Farmers Weekly *of 1946. Farmers' wives were invited to send in their recipes, many of which had been passed down for generations and were known only to them. Quite a few recipes included oatmeal, both as a filler and as a substitute for flour.*

Oats and oatmeal stem from the time of the Greeks and Romans who regarded them as suitable food for their animals. However, the Romans encouraged the growing of oats in Britain and it became a popular food in Ireland, Wales and Scotland, where the climate and terrain favoured its growth rather than the other cereals. But the wealthier households in England shunned oats and it remained the food of the poor until the health-giving properties of oatmeal were discovered.

Roll out the pastry on a lightly floured surface sprinkled with 25g (1 oz) oatmeal and use it to line a deep 23cm (9 in) tart tin. Prick the base all over using a fork, brush with egg white and pre-bake in the oven for 20 minutes as directed on page 16. Pre-heat the oven to 200°C/400°F/Gas 6.

Meanwhile, peel, core and thinly slice the apples and put them in a saucepan with the cider or water. Add the cloves and cinnamon. Cover, bring to the boil, then reduce the heat and simmer gently for about 5 minutes or until the apples are just tender but not mushy. Remove the apple slices using a slotted spoon, then drain. Bubble the liquid in the saucepan for a further 10 minutes or until it reduces and thickens a little. Arrange the apple slices in a ring on the base of the pre-baked pastry case, then cover with the thickened liquid. Top with the knobs of butter and sprinkle over the sugar.

Mix the breadcrumbs and remaining oatmeal with the sultanas and sprinkle on top. Pour the golden syrup over the filling. Bake in the oven for 25–30 minutes or until the top looks scrunchy and golden brown.

SERVE warm or cold with some extra thick double cream.

COOK'S TIP – Miss Hughes, who sent this tart recipe to *Farmers Weekly*, claimed that 'the tart, when it is cold, is solid and carries well in a tin.'

Gooseberry and Marshmallow Lattice Tart

SERVES 6–8

225g (8 oz) rich sweet shortcrust pastry (see page 15)

675g (1½ lb) gooseberries (canned or frozen gooseberries may be used, if fresh ones are not available – see Cook's Tip)

175g (6 oz) demerara sugar

juice of ½ lemon

½ teaspoon ground cinnamon

2 egg yolks, beaten

beaten egg, to glaze

about 5 marshmallows

This tart has a very simple recipe with a play on the word mallow. As far back as the Middle Ages, the marsh mallow – a common purple flowering plant related to the hollyhock – was a highly valued herb. It was said to withstand all the evils of witchcraft and was used to protect the skin by mashing the herb together with egg white. It is from this paste that we get the term marshmallow – the synthetic and very modern sweet used here. I hope this somewhat tacky twentieth-century decoration is excused on the grounds that the tart looks good on the table.

Line a deep 23cm (9 in) tart tin with the pastry (leave a few strips of pastry for the lattice) and pre-bake or bake blind as directed on page 16. Pre-heat the oven to 220°C/425°F/Gas 7.

Top and tail the gooseberries and wash and drain them in a colander. Place the gooseberries in a heavy-bottomed pan with enough water to cover. Add the sugar and cook gently for about 10 minutes or until the gooseberries are soft, stirring occasionally. Add the lemon juice and cinnamon and give the mixture a light mashing up with a fork or potato masher. Remove the pan from the heat and set aside to cool.

Mix the egg yolks into the gooseberry mixture. Place the mixture in the pre-baked pastry case, then top the tart with the reserved pastry strips to make a lattice. Brush the lattice strips lightly with beaten egg. Bake in the oven for 20–25 minutes, or until the lattice strips are golden brown. Remove the tart from the oven. Pre-heat the grill to high.

Prepare the marshmallows by slicing them in half so that they are quite thin (trim the edges if they are a bit large). Place one in each square provided by the lattice on top of the tart. Place the tart under the hot grill, just long enough to brown the tops of the marshmallows.

SERVE hot or warm with thick cream.

COOK'S TIP – When using canned or frozen gooseberries, the amount of sugar used and the cooking time should be reduced. This will depend on how firm and sweet the fruit seems when you test it before cooking.

Prune and Almond Crumble Tart

SERVES 8

175g (6 oz) rich sweet shortcrust pastry
(see page 15)

FOR THE PRUNE BASE:

two 250g (9 oz) packets ready-to-eat
pitted dried prunes

375ml (13 fl oz) red wine

pared strip of orange rind

1 cinnamon stick

2 cloves

75ml (2½ fl oz) port, sherry or marsala

FOR THE CRUMBLE:

55g (2 oz) ground almonds

½ teaspoon ground cinnamon

½ teaspoon ground mace or
grated nutmeg

115g (4 oz) light soft brown sugar

175g (6 oz) plain flour

115g (4 oz) cold, unsalted butter,
chopped into small pieces

25g (1 oz) almonds, finely chopped

sifted icing sugar, mixed with a little
grated nutmeg, to decorate

*T*he term prune (French for plum) has been used since medieval times to describe a dried plum. Although tainted with childhood jokes, the prune is making a comeback. This is partly the result of the wider availability of dried prunes, particularly the succulent Prune d'Agen from Aquitaine, which was an important export from France to California in the nineteenth century.

The prune is well known in descriptions of old tarts, principally as the key ingredient of 'black tart stuff' described by Elizabeth David. Prunes go well with meats (such as sausages), and there are several recipes for prune and egg custard tarts.

The tart described here, however, is more akin to the seventeenth-century 'black tart' and can at the same time be viewed as the early predecessor of the famous American 'shoo-fly pie' (so-called because flies were attracted to the pie when it was taken out of the oven).

Crumbles as we know them today did not really appear widely until the 1939–45 war as an austerity practice to make food go further. So this tart has a very mixed heritage.

Line a shallow 23cm (9 in) tart tin with the pastry and pre-bake or bake blind as directed on page 16. Pre-heat the oven to 200°C/400°F/Gas 6.

Put the prunes, red wine, 300ml (½ pint) water, the orange rind, spices and port or sherry in a heavy-bottomed saucepan, stir to mix, then bring to the boil. Cover and simmer gently for about 20 minutes or until the prunes are well plumped up and nicely spiced, stirring occasionally. Ideally, you want a fairly sloppy mixture and so it might be worth heating it further and reducing the liquid down a bit, if the mixture is still too runny. Remove and discard the orange rind, cinnamon stick and cloves.

Meanwhile, make the crumble topping, putting all the crumble ingredients together in a bowl and rubbing in the butter, making sure it is mixed in well and quickly.

Assemble the tart by putting the prune mixture in the pre-baked pastry case, then spoon the crumble mixture evenly over the top. Bake in the oven for 30–35 minutes. Check that the crumble is not getting too dark brown; if it is, put a loose layer of foil over the top. Remove the tart from the oven and allow it to cool. Dust with sifted icing sugar mixed with nutmeg just before serving.

SERVE warm with vanilla custard.

COOK'S TIP – Ideally you should prepare your prunes one day before making this tart, but some of the supermarket dried prunes are so succulent and tender nowadays that there is really no need for soaking.

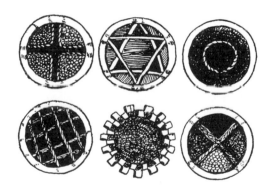

Date and Walnut Toffee Tart

SERVES 6–8

350g (12 oz) rich sweet shortcrust pastry
  (see page 15)

225g (8 oz) caster sugar

170g (6 oz) can evaporated milk

55g (2 oz) butter

90ml (3 fl oz) double cream

175g (6 oz) walnuts, finely chopped

55g (2 oz) dried dates, chopped

55g (2 oz) ready-to-eat dried prunes,
  chopped

115g (4 oz) icing sugar

The walnut tree did not come to Britain until the fifteenth century, our often cold and wet climate seeming too hostile for such a southern European tree, but it flourished, nevertheless, particularly on large estates. Some of the latter specialised in different species of walnut and at Wimpole Hall, a National Trust house just outside Cambridge, they grew 40 different varieties.

Recipes using walnuts appeared in Britain in the seventeenth century and it became a favourite in puddings and pies, often mixed with cinnamon, eggs, sugar and cream. The walnut regained prominence in the mid-twentieth century with the popularity of the Waldorf salad.

This tart is based on an early nineteenth-century recipe with a 1950s twist of using evaporated milk.

Roll out 175g (6 oz) pastry on a lightly floured surface and use it to line a shallow 23cm (9 in) tart tin. Pre-bake or bake blind as directed on page 16. Wrap and chill the remaining pastry. Pre-heat the oven to 170°C/325°F/Gas 3.

Put the caster sugar and 2 tablespoons water in a wide, heavy-bottomed frying pan or saucepan and heat gently until the sugar has dissolved, stirring constantly, then bring to the boil and boil very gently, stirring, until it is golden brown. Remove the pan from the heat and quickly stir in the evaporated milk, butter and cream before the sugar mixture sets. The mixture may be lumpy – it will certainly be runny and pale gold in colour – but will not look like toffee. Put the pan back on a low heat and stir carefully – the heat will make it start to thicken and turn a rich golden brown. When the residual mark of the spoon stays in the 'toffee' then take the pan off the heat and allow it to cool for 15 minutes or so.

Put the walnuts, dates and prunes in the pastry case and spoon the cooled toffee on top.

Roll out the remaining pastry to make a lid and place it on top of the tart, pressing the edges to seal. Make one or two slashes in the lid, then place the tart in the oven and bake for 30 minutes or until set and golden brown. Remove the tart from the oven and let it cool.

Mix the sifted icing sugar in a bowl with 2 tablespoons hot water, to make an icing. Drizzle the icing across the top of the tart in a haphazard manner.

SERVE at room temperature or cold on its own.

COOK'S TIP – This tart doesn't really need anything to go with it, although the sharpness of crème fraîche is better than ordinary cream, if you must succumb.

A School Custard Tart

SERVES 10

225g (8 oz) rich sweet shortcrust pastry
   (see page 15)
400g (14 oz) can condensed milk
300ml (½ pint) hot milk
½ teaspoon salt
½ teaspoon vanilla essence
3 eggs, well-beaten
¼ whole fresh nutmeg

This tart is for those who like to raid the fridge late at night. Condensed milk was invented in Victorian times and travelled the world during the days of the British Empire, brightening the lives of the many British expatriates stranded in tropical lands where safe fresh milk was unobtainable. In more recent times, it underwent a wartime revival, becoming 'comfort food' for children of all ages in the 1940s. It often found its way into school tarts, and this is one of them. It is very easy to make and is heartily disapproved of by 'proper' cooks.

Line a deep 23cm (9 in) tart tin with the pastry and pre-bake or bake blind as directed on page 16. Pre-heat the oven to 200°C/400°F/Gas 6.

Put the condensed milk, hot milk, salt and vanilla essence in a large bowl and stir to mix. The condensed milk will melt into the hot milk. Add the eggs and mix well. Pour the mixture into the pre-baked pastry case and grate the piece of nutmeg over the top of the custard mixture. Bake in the oven for 10 minutes, then reduce the oven temperature to 170°C/325°F/Gas 3 and bake the tart for a further 30–35 minutes or until the filling begins to firm up. Test with a knife to see if it is sufficiently cooked before removing the tart from the oven.

SERVE warm or cold, especially late at night.

Burnt Sugar Lemon Tart

SERVES 6

225g (8 oz) rich sweet shortcrust pastry (see page 15)

finely grated zest and juice of 5 large lemons

115g (4 oz) caster sugar

2 teaspoons brandy or sherry

225ml (8 fl oz) double cream

4 eggs, plus 4 egg yolks

sifted icing sugar, for sprinkling on top

We associate lemons with the Mediterranean lands but they originated in northern India and only reached the Mediterranean in the first century AD, appearing in many Roman recipes and found in archaeological remains. Their transfer to northern Europe was slow and although it bucked up a bit in the late Middle Ages their use was still confined to the wealthy.

Lemon tarts became more common in the seventeenth and eighteenth centuries, many of them being very rich with the addition of cream and eggs; and most of us are familiar with the lemon meringue pie.

This particular lemon tart is very simple and good to look at with its earthy last-minute grilling, and it is flexible in how it can be served.

Line a deep 23cm (9 in) tart tin with the pastry and pre-bake or bake blind as directed on page 16. Pre-heat the oven to 200°C/400°F/Gas 6. Pre-heat a baking sheet in the oven until warm.

Put the lemon zest and juice, caster sugar and brandy or sherry in a bowl and stir to mix. Slowly beat in the cream, followed by the eggs and egg yolks (one at a time). Put the pre-baked pastry case on the warmed baking sheet and pour the lemon liquid into the tart case. Place the tart on the baking sheet in the centre of the oven. Bake for 25–30 minutes or until the filling is just set. If the edges of the pastry begin to colour too much and too quickly (have a look after about 15 minutes), cover the edges with some crinkled foil edging.

When cooked, remove the tart from the oven and pre-heat the grill to high. Sprinkle the tart with icing sugar and place under the hot grill until lightly browned. If you prefer, you can allow the tart to cool and then sprinkle it with icing sugar without putting it under the grill.

SERVE hot, warm or cold with a dollop of fresh cream or crème fraîche.

COOK'S TIP – This tart also goes well with raspberries, strawberries or blueberries. If you want to make it special, decorate the baked cool tart with fresh fruit (halved in the case of strawberries) and then sprinkle with icing sugar, but don't put it under the grill!

Lemon Meringue Tart

SERVES 6–8

1 Burnt Sugar Lemon Tart
    (see page 117)

4 egg whites

225g (8 oz) caster sugar

There are so many recipes around for the very popular Lemon Meringue Tart (or Pie) that I thought at first of not including it here, even though it is a tart well known to and loved by our grandparents. However, I thought it was worth including this particular recipe, not only because it is rich and satisfying, but also because it can be converted quite easily from the Burnt Sugar Lemon Tart (see page 117).

Follow the instructions for making the Burnt Sugar Lemon Tart (see page 117 but without decorating it). Allow it to cool.

Reduce the oven temperature to 180°C/350°F/Gas 4.

Whisk the egg whites in a large bowl until they are at the soft peaks stage. Whisk in 115g (4 oz) sugar in 2–3 batches, then fold in the remaining caster sugar using a metal spoon. Spread the meringue over the cooling lemon tart, making sure it goes right up to the pastry edges. Fluff up the meringue with a fork. Bake in the oven for 15–20 minutes, or until the meringue is crisp and golden.

SERVE warm or cold with cream or ice cream.

Plum and Almond Tart

SERVES 6–8

one 375g (13 oz) packet chilled ready-
    made puff pastry

a little sifted icing sugar, for rolling out

one 250g (9 oz) packet marzipan

675g (1½ lb) large ripe plums, halved
    and stoned

2 tablespoons brandy

½ teaspoon almond essence

25g (1 oz) light soft brown sugar

¼ teaspoon ground cinnamon

25g (1 oz) butter, cut into small pieces

Continuing the theme of the contented marriage between plum and almond, this tart is simplicity itself. Fashionable in its use of a square puff pastry base, it can be produced in just a few minutes.

Pre-heat the oven to 190°C/375°F/Gas 5. Place a baking sheet in the oven to get hot.

Roll out the pastry on a lightly floured surface into a free-form rectangular shape about 46 x 20cm (18 x 8 in) in size and prick all over with a fork. Using a sharp knife, score a line 2.5cm (1 in) from the edges of the pastry, all around the case, to encourage the pastry to puff up even more and form a border when baked.

Lightly dust the work surface with icing sugar, roll out the marzipan until quite thin, then place it on top of the pastry, leaving the pastry border uncovered. Cover the marzipan with the plums, cut-side down.

Mix the brandy in a bowl with the almond essence and splash the mixture over the plums.

Combine the soft brown sugar with the cinnamon and sprinkle over the plums.

Put the pieces of butter, evenly spaced, on top of the plums. Carefully transfer the tart on to the hot baking sheet in the oven and bake for 35–40 minutes or until golden. The pastry will puff up, leaving the tender plums resting in a tasty, dark almondy juice. If the pastry border becomes too brown while cooking, cover it with a strip of foil.

SERVE hot, warm or cold with crème fraîche.

A Modern Apple Tart

SERVES 6–8

175g (6 oz) rich sweet shortcrust pastry
(see page 15)
85g (3 oz) caster sugar
25g (1 oz) plain flour
4 large Bramley apples
juice of ½ lemon (optional)
85g (3 oz) light soft brown sugar
300ml (½ pint) single cream
a little grated nutmeg, to decorate

This is the simplest yet most delicious way to cook apples, one which was used by the earliest cooks. The sharpness of the apples is countered by the rich butter coating and the emphasis is on the excellence of the ingredients, especially the pastry. The thin apple slices look particularly good in a square or narrow rectangular tart tin, if you have one. The quantities given are for a shallow 23cm (9 in) round tart tin, but adaptability is the key here.

Line a shallow 23cm (9 in) tart tin with the pastry and pre-bake or bake blind as directed on page 16. Pre-heat the oven to 190°C/375°F/Gas 5.

Peel and core the apples, then slice them very thinly. If you are worried about discoloration, sprinkle the apple slices with the lemon juice.

Put the caster sugar and flour in a large bowl. Place the apple slices in the bowl and toss to coat them well with flour and sugar. Remove the apple slices from the flour mixture, shake off any excess, then arrange them in the pre-baked pastry case, leaning, overlapping and with their curved edges uppermost, in concentric circles around the tart (if you are using a round tart tin) or in straight rows (if you are using a rectangular tart tin). Bake in the oven for about 15–20 minutes, or until the apple slices have started to become juicy.

Remove the tart from the oven and sprinkle most of the soft brown sugar over the apples, then pour the cream over the top. Sprinkle on the remaining soft brown sugar. Put the tart back in the oven and bake for a further 20–25 minutes or until it is nicely browned, being careful to protect the pastry edges by covering them with foil, if necessary, to prevent over-browning. Remove the tart from the oven and sprinkle with a little grated nutmeg.

SERVE hot or cold, on its own, or with vanilla ice cream.

A Modern Mixed-berry Tart

SERVES 6–8

175g (6 oz) rich sweet shortcrust pastry
(see page 15)

2 tablespoons plain flour

115g (4 oz) caster sugar

finely grated zest of ½ lemon

large pinch of ground cinnamon

675g (1½ lb) mixed fresh berries, such as
raspberries, blackberries and
blueberries

115g (4 oz) dark chocolate

175g (6 oz) stale Madeira or sponge
cake, crumbled

a little icing sugar, to decorate

There is something magical about a medley of mixed berries in a jelly, pudding or tart. And the spirits rise when you realise how easy it is to produce something so delightful and mouthwatering with ease and pleasure. You can use any mix of berries you like – and other soft fruit like redcurrants and blackcurrants fit in very well. You may also wish to produce tartlets rather than one large tart, in which case reduce the cooking time by about 10 minutes.

Line a shallow 23cm (9 in) tart tin with the pastry and pre-bake or bake blind as directed on page 16. Pre-heat the oven to 190°C/375°F/Gas 5.

Place the flour, caster sugar, lemon zest, cinnamon and fruit in a bowl, and mix well.

Grate the chocolate into a separate bowl, add the crumbled-up cake, mix well, then sprinkle the mixture over the base of the pre-baked pastry case.

Arrange the fruit mixture on top, then bake in the oven for 25–30 minutes or until the fruit is syrupy and bubbling. Remove the tart from the oven and allow it to cool for a while, then sprinkle the tart with sifted icing sugar.

SERVE warm or at room temperature with single cream or crème fraîche.

COOK'S TIP – Variations include (i) sprinkling 55g (2 oz) mixed ground almonds and some other chopped nuts over the pastry base before covering with fruit; (ii) omit the cake and chocolate and use just the fruit (but rather more of it), and to eat the baked tart cold; (iii) prepare a fruit glaze by heating up 100g (3½ oz) redcurrant jelly and pouring it over the fruit through a sieve. Let it cool before serving.

Apple Butterscotch Crumble Tart

SERVES 6–8

225g (8 oz) rich sweet shortcrust pastry
  (see page 15)
175g (6 oz) self-raising flour (or half
  wholemeal and half white self-raising
  flour)
55g (2 oz) oats
2 teaspoons ground cinnamon
115g (4 oz) demerara sugar
140g (5 oz) cold unsalted butter, diced
  into small cubes
115g (4 oz) butter
115g (4 oz) light soft brown sugar
900g (2 lb) eating apples (preferably
  Cox's Orange Pippins), peeled, cored
  and thinly sliced
finely grated zest of 1 orange
85g (3 oz) raisins
a little demerara sugar, to sprinkle
  (optional)

The wide use of the crumble during the last World War enabled cooks to display imagination and creativity with the humblest of fare. Windfalls and the shelves of wrinkled apples on yellowing newspaper provoked even the most culinarily challenged housewife to reach for the margarine and dried oats, producing a rich and irresistible dish crowded with memories and promise.

In the interests of luxury, I have substituted good quality butter for the wartime economy margarine.

Line a deep 23cm (9 in) tart tin with the pastry and pre-bake or bake blind as directed on page 16. Pre-heat the oven to 190°C/375°F/Gas 5.

Prepare the crumble first, as it turns out more crunchy if it can enjoy a few minutes' rest in the freezer before cooking. Mix together the flour, oats, cinnamon and sugar in a bowl. Rub in the butter for just a minute or two until partly absorbed and the mixture is beginning to stick. Place the bowl in the freezer until you have made the filling.

Melt the butter and soft brown sugar in a heavy-bottomed frying pan over a low heat. Add the apple slices. Cover and cook them in the buttery sauce for a few minutes – just enough to enable the apples to soften, stirring occasionally. Remove the pan from the heat, add the orange zest and raisins, stir to mix, then pour the mixture into the pre-baked pastry case. Cover the buttery apples with the crumble mixture. If you wish, you can sprinkle with a little demerara sugar. Bake in the oven for 50–55 minutes or until brown and the fruit juices are oozing up around the edges.

SERVE hot or warm with good dairy ice cream or crème fraîche.

Stepmother's Tart

SERVES 6–8

175g (6 oz) rich sweet shortcrust pastry
(see page 15)

25g (1 oz) unsalted butter

2 tablespoons light soft brown sugar

450g (1 lb) ready-to-eat dried apricots

2 tablespoons amaretto

55g (2 oz) almonds, finely chopped

3 egg yolks

85g (3 oz) caster sugar

175ml (6 fl oz) double cream

½ teaspoon almond essence

sifted icing sugar and a few roughly
chopped almonds, to decorate

*T*his tart is something of an indulgence on my part – to remind me of my early days as a stepmother by bringing together a mixture of favourite ingredients under one roof, as it were. Stepmothers have a poor culinary heritage, often being accused of neglectful behaviour towards their charges; and I cannot pretend that this tart has any long-standing traditions attached to it.

But perhaps this contribution, developed some 30 years ago, might one day enter the annals of historical tart-making. I hope its caramelly, fruity, nutty and creamy filling will do much to enhance the reputation of stepmothers throughout the land. It is similar to Tarte Grandmère, but much tastier, I think.

Line a shallow 23cm (9 in) tart tin with the pastry and pre-bake or bake blind as directed on page 16. Pre-heat the oven to 180°C/350°F/Gas 4.

Melt the butter and sugar in a heavy-bottomed or non-stick saucepan until blended and light golden brown in colour, stirring occasionally. Add the apricots and cook for 2–3 minutes so that they are all well coated in the butter mixture, stirring occasionally. Cover the apricots with water, add the amaretto, cover, bring to the boil, then reduce the heat and simmer until the apricots are really tender, stirring occasionally. Keep the apricots just covered with water and top up as necessary. Remove the pan from the heat and mash the mixture a little with a potato masher, draining off any excess liquid so that the end result is an apricot goo. Spoon the apricot mixture in the pre-baked pastry case. Sprinkle the chopped almonds over the top, then put to one side.

Whisk the egg yolks and sugar together in a bowl until pale and shiny. Add the cream and almond essence and mix well. Spoon the egg mixture evenly over the apricot. Bake in the oven for 40–45 minutes or until well-browned and set. Remove the tart from the oven and allow to cool. Once cool, dust the tart with sifted icing sugar and sprinkle with a few chopped almonds.

SERVE either warm or cold with single cream or crème fraîche.

COOK'S TIP – This tart is also solid enough to take on picnics.

A MELODY OF MODERN OLD TARTS

While I have been writing this book, the tart has undergone something of a transformation with a regular stream of articles and enticing photographs. At the same time, more ready-made tarts, both savoury and sweet, are appearing on supermarket shelves. This is heartening news for all tart lovers and justifies this end-piece dedication to the modern tart. The general theme of this recent wave of appreciation for the tart is simplicity, but a simplicity based on the very best of ingredients.

Purists may argue that it is the quality of the pastry that makes a good tart and this is particularly true when the filling is without adornment. So, for those who have been straining at the bit to practise their own favoured version of pastry, now is their opportunity.

Interestingly, the modern tart is exemplifying the very essence of early tart-making – with its preference for an unstructured or linear shape, its use of fresh fruit and the return of almonds, honey, spices and alcohol. So, as you bake these tarts do not feel that you are in any sense betraying traditions of any kind – they can compete with the very best of the old tarts.

BIBLIOGRAPHY

In researching the origins of these old tarts I found some books became my constant companions. The most important were: *The Oxford Companion to Food* edited by Alan Davidson, *Food and Drink in Britain*, by C. Anne Wilson, *Food in England* by Dorothy Hartley, *Wild Food* by Roger Phillips, *A Taste of History* produced by English Heritage and *Seven Centuries of English Cooking* by Maxine de la Falaise. I am also indebted to other cookery writers, especially the many excellent authors of books of modern tarts, and I hope I have included them all here.

HISTORICAL BOOKS (BRITISH COOKING TRADITIONS AND RECIPES)

Apicus, *The Roman Cookery Book*, George C. Harrap & Co Ltd, London 1958

Ayrton, Elizabeth, *The Cookery of England*, Penguin Books, Harmondsworth 1977

Berriedale-Johnson, Michelle, *Olde Englishe Recipes*, Piatkus, London 1981

Black, Maggie, Jane Renfrew and others, *A Taste of History*, English Heritage in association with the British Museum Press, London 1993

Beeton, Mrs , *Beeton's Book of Household Management* Isabella (ed.), facsimile edition, Jonathan Cape, London 1968

Craig, Elizabeth, *Court Favourites*, Andre Deutsch, London 1953

Davies, Jennifer, *The Victorian Kitchen*, BBC Books, London 1989

Day, Ivan (ed.), *Eat, Drink and Be Merry – the British at Table, 1600–2000*, Philip Wilson, London 2000

Drummond, J.C. and Wilbraham, Anne, *The Englishman's Food*, Jonathan Cape, London, 1969

Falaise, Maxime de la, *Seven Centuries of English Cooking*, Weidenfeld and Nicolson, London 1973

Fitzgibbon, Theodora, *The Art of British Cooking*, Robert Hale Ltd, London 1965

Glasse, Hannah, *The Art of Cookery Made Plain and Easy (by a lady)*, republished, Prospect Books, 1995

Grigson, J., *English Food*, Macmillan, London 1974

Harlan Hale, William, *The Horizon Cookbook and Illustrated History of Eating and Drinking Through the Ages*, American Heritage Publishing Co Inc, New York 1985

Hartley, Dorothy, *Food in England*, Macdonald, London 1954

Hutchins, Sheila, *English Recipes as They Appeared in Eighteenth and Nineteenth Century Cookery Books*, Methuen, London 1967

Nilsen, Angela and June Weatherall (eds), *Just Like Mother Used to Make*, Circle Books, 1973

Sambrook, Pamela and Peter Brears (eds), *The Country House Kitchen 1650–1900*, Sutton Publishing in association with The National Trust, London 1997

Shephard, Sue, *Pickled, Potted and Canned – The Story of Food Preserving*, Headline, London 2000

Toussaint-Samat, Maguelonne, *A History of Food*, Blackwell, Oxford 1992

GENERAL COOKERY BOOKS

Berry, Mary, *Mary Berry's New Aga Cookbook*, Headline, London 1999

Boxer, Arabella, *Book of English Food*, Hodder and Stoughton, London 1991

Braimbridge, Sophie, *Quick and Easy Dairy Cooking*, J. Sainsbury, London 1997

Campbell, Susan, *English Cookery, New and Old, 1931*, (Consumers' Association), Hodder and Stoughton, London 1981

Carrier, Robert, *Cooking for You*, Hamlyn, London 1970

Conil, Jean, *The Home Cookery Book*, Methuen, London 1956

Costa, Margaret, *Four Seasons Cookery Book*, Sphere, London 1970

David, Elizabeth, *An Omelette and a Glass of Wine*, (a Jill Norman book), Robert Hale Ltd, London 1952

Davidson, Alan (ed), *The Oxford Companion to Food*, Oxford University Press, Oxford 1999

Davies, Gilli, *The Very Best Flavours of Wales*, Gomer, Llandysul 1997

Dimbleby, Josceline, *Book of Puddings, Desserts and Savouries*, Hodder and Stoughton, London 1979

Farmhouse Fare, Country Recipes Collected by the Farmers Weekly, Hulton Press Ltd, London 1946

Freud, Clement, *Freud on Food*, Dent, London 1978

Good Housekeeping, *English Recipes Old and New*, National Magazine Co Ltd, London 1959

Good Housekeeping, *New Picture Cookery*, National Magazine Co Ltd, London 1966

Heath, Ambrose, *Good Sweets*, Faber and Faber, London 1937

Heaton, Nell, *Traditional Recipes of the British Isles*, Faber and Faber, London 1950

Lawrence, Sue, *Scots Cooking*, Headline, London 2000

Lawson, Nigella, *How to be a Domestic Goddess*, Chatto and Windus, London 2000

Lawson, Nigella, *How to Eat*, Chatto and Windus, London 1998

Phillips, Roger, *Wild Food*, Pan Books, London 1983

Rance, Patrick, *The Great British Cheese Book*, Macmillan, London 1982

Rhodes, Gary, *Sweet Dreams*, Hodder and Stoughton, London 1998

Rubinstein and Bush, *The Penguin Freezer Cook Book*, Penguin Books, London 1973

Slater, Nigel, *Nigel Slater's Real Food*, Fourth Estate, London 2000

Smith, Delia, *How to Cook, Book One*, BBC Worldwide, London 1998

Smith, Michael, *Fine English Cookery*, Faber and Faber, London 1972

Spry, Constance and Hume, Rosemary, *The Constance Spry Cookery Book*, Dent, London 1956

BOOKS ON PASTRY, TARTS AND PIES

Berenbaum, Rose Levy, *The Pie and Pastry Bible*, Scribner, New York 1998

Collister, Linda, *Sweet Pies & Tarts*, Ryland Peters & Small, London 1997

Dannenberg, Linda, *French Tarts*, Artisan, New York 1997

Day-Lewis, Tamasin, *The Art of the Tart*, Cassell & Co, London 2000

Elliot, Rose, *Rose Elliott's Book of Savoury Flans and Pies*, Fontana Paperback, London 1984

Good Housekeeping, *Perfect Pastry (the cookeen edition)*, National Magazine Co Ltd, London 1984

Le Cordon Bleu, *Tarts and Pastries*, Merehurst, London 1998

McNair, James, *Pie Cookbook*, Rockpile Press, San Francisco 1989

Thompson, Sylvia, *Festive Tarts*, Chronicle Books, San Francisco 1996

Willan, Anne, *Perfect Pies and Tarts*, Dorling Kindersley, London 1997

Williams-Sonoma, *Pies and Tarts*, Weldon Owen, San Francisco 1992

Wolf-Cohen, Elizabeth, *Simple Tarts*, Apple Books, 1996

INDEX

Ale, Spiced Dried-fruit Tart
    Cooked in 45
almonds 9
    Almond Cream Custard
        Tart 42
    Apricot and Almond
        Tart 34
    Baked Almond Tart
        with Nutmeg and Sweet
        Wine 46
    Congress Tartlets 53
    Fig, Thyme, Honey and
        Almond Tart 44
    Gooseberry, Elderflower
        and Almond Tart 81
    Maid of Honour Tartlets 55
    Orange and Lemon Almond
        Tart 35
    Plum and Almond Tart 119
    Plum Tart with a Rich
        Almond Custard 74
    Prune and Almond Crumble
        Tart 112-13
    see also Bakewell Tarts
Anchovy and Sorrel Tart 22
apples
    Apple Butterscotch
        Crumble Tart 122
    Apple Snow Dumpling Tart
        38-9
    Blackberry and Apple
        Butterscotch Tart 58-9
    Canterbury Pudding Tart 84
    Fidget Pie 62-3
    A Modern Apple Tart 120
    Oatmeal, Apple and Syrup
        Tart 110
    Pumpkin and Apple Tart 49
apricots
    Apricot and Almond Tart 34
    Dried Apricot Tart 54
    Stepmother's Tart 123
Artichoke Tart, Pea and 28
Asparagus and Butter Cream
    Tart 72

bacon
    Fidget Pie 62-3
    Welsh Leek, Bacon and
        Goat's Cheese Tart 100
Bakewell Tarts 77-80, 103
Banana, Butter and Meringue
    Tart 106-7
Beer, Rhubarb and Strawberry
    Tart Cooked in 90-1
Bilberry 'Mucky Mouth' Tart 86
Blackberry and Apple
    Butterscotch Tart 58-9
Bread and Butter Pudding Tart
    92
Broad Bean Tart, Seventeenth-
    century 29
Burnt Cream Tart 96-7
Burnt Sugar Lemon Tart 117
Buttermilk Raisin Tart 36

Canterbury Pudding Tart 84
Carrot and Cumin Tart 30
Chaucer's Sweet Garlic and
    Herb Tart 27
cheese
    Courgette, Garlic and Blue
        Cheese Tart 101
    Eighteenth-century Three-
        cheese Tart 65
    Lovage, Tomato and Cheese
        Tart 25
    Maid of Honour Tartlets 55
    A Medieval Tart of Brie 24
    Sambocade 43
    A Sixteenth-century Tart of
        Flowers 56
    Stilton and Parsnip Tart 69
    Tomato, Onion and Goat's
        Cheese Tart 66-7
    Welsh Leek, Bacon and
        Goat's Cheese Tart 100
    Yorkshire Curd Tart 87
Cherry Tart 48
Chestnut and Chocolate Raisin
    Tart 75
Chocolate Tart 82

Chocolate Tart, A 1960s Pear
    and 108-9
Congress Tartlets 53
Courgette, Garlic and Blue
    Cheese Tart 101
Cumbrian Tart 103
Custard Tarts 40-1, 47, 50-1,
    116

Date and Walnut Toffee Tart
    114-15
decoration 10, 17, 19

Eighteenth-century Three-
    cheese Tart 65
Elderflower and Almond Tart,
    Gooseberry, 81
Elderflower Cream Cheese Tart
    (Sambocade) 43
equipment 14, 16

Fidget (Fitchet or Figet) Pie 62-3
Fig, Thyme, Honey and Almond
    Tart 44
fish and seafood
    Anchovy and Sorrel Tart 22
    Roman Seafood Tart 20
    Salmon and Herb Tart 23
    Scottish Smoked Salmon
        and Cucumber Cream
        Cheese Tart 21
    Smoked Haddock Tart 64
flowers 10, 19, 56
freezing 18

Garlic and Blue Cheese Tart,
    Courgette, 101
Garlic and Herb Tart, Chaucer's
    Sweet 27
glaze 17
Gooseberry, Elderflower and
    Almond Tart 81
Gooseberry and Marshmallow
    Lattice Tart 111

Grandmother's Tart 37

Harlequin Tart 76
Hazelnut Tart, Peach and 57
herbs 8
    Chaucer's Sweet Garlic and
    Herb Tart 27
    Fresh Herb Tart 26
    Salmon and Herb Tart 23
history 7-12, 19, 60-1, 98

Irish Creamy Potato and
    Rocket Tart 73

Lancaster Tart 80
Leek and Mushroom Tart 32
Leek, Bacon and Goat's
    Cheese Tart, Welsh 100
lemons
    Burnt Sugar Lemon Tart 117
    Lancaster Tart 80
    Lemon Meringue Tart 118
    Lemon Pudding Tart 83
    Orange and Lemon Almond
    Tart 35
Lord Woolton Pie 102
Lovage, Tomato and Cheese
    Tart 25

Maid of Honour Tartlets 55
Manchester Tart 94-5
Medieval Tart of Brie 24
Mixed-berry Tart, A Modern
    121
Mushroom Tart, Leek and 32
Mustard Tart, Sausage and 99

Norfolk Treacle Tart 89
Nutmeg and Sweet Wine,
    Baked Almond Tart with 46

Oatmeal, Apple and Syrup Tart
    110
Onion Tart 31
Orange and Lemon Almond
    Tart 35

Parsnip Tart, Stilton and 69
pastry 13-18
    baking 'blind' and pre-
    baking 16
    history 8-9, 10
    old-world variations 17
    plain shortcrust 15
    rich sweet shortcrust (pâte
    brisée) 15
Pea and Artichoke Tart 28
Peach and Hazelnut Tart 57
Pear and Chocolate Tart, A
    1960s 108-9
Pine Nut and Cream Tart 37
Plum and Almond Tart 119
Plum Tart with a Rich Almond
    Custard 74
Potato and Rocket Tart, Irish
    Creamy 73
Potato Tart, Spinach, Raisin
    and 70-1
Prune and Almond Crumble
    Tart 112-13
Pumpkin and Apple Tart 49

Quince Custard Tart 40-1

Raisin, Orange and Cinnamon
    Tart 93
Raisin Tart, Buttermilk 36
Raisin Tart, Chestnut and
    Chocolate 75
Raspberry and Rice Pudding
    Tart 85
Raspberry Cream Tart 52

Rhubarb and Strawberry Tart
    Cooked in Beer 90-1
Rice Pudding Tart, Raspberry
    and 85
Rice Tart 33
Roman Seafood Tart 20

Salmon and Herb Tart 23
Sambocade 43
Sausage and Mustard Tart 99
School Custard Tart, A 116
Scottish Smoked Salmon and
    Cucumber Cream Cheese
    Tart 21
Seventeenth-century Broad
    Bean Tart 29
Sixteenth-century Tart of
    Flowers, A 56
Smoked Haddock Tart 64
Spiced Dried-fruit Tart Cooked
    in Ale 45
Spinach, Raisin and Potato Tart
    70-1
Stepmother's Tart 123
Stilton and Parsnip Tart 69
Strawberry and Verjuice
    Custard Tart 50-1
Strawberry Tart Cooked in
    Beer, Rhubarb and 90-1
Sultana Meringue Tart 104-5

Tomato, Onion and Goat's
    Cheese Tart 66-7
Treacle Tarts 88-9

Walnut Tart, Pickled 68
Walnut Toffee Tart, Date and
    114-15
Welsh Leek, Bacon and Goat's
    Cheese Tart 100

Yorkshire Curd Tart 87